The LORD is KING

To the members of North Arbury Chapel,
Cambridge, 1976–1989, in the freedom of whose
fellowship it was always possible to think.

The LORD _is_ KING

REDISCOVERING FREEDOM

HUGH WILLIAMSON

CROSSWAY BOOKS

CROSSWAY BOOKS
38 De Montfort Street, Leicester LE1 7GP, England

© Hugh Williamson 1993, 1997

First published under the title Jesus is Lord *in 1993*
This edition published in 1997

British Library Cataloguing in Publication Data
A catalogue record for this book is available from the British Library.

ISBN 1-85684-166-9

Set in Garamond

Typeset in Great Britain by Parker Typesetting Service, Leicester
Printed and bound in Great Britain by
The Guernsey Press Co. Ltd., Guernsey, Channel Islands

CONTENTS

FOREWORD 6

1 MUST WE BE NOBODY? 7

2 BUT DEATH IS THE END, ISN'T IT? 14

3 JESUS' DEATH: THE BEGINNING 21

4 THE IDOL OF GLOBAL ECONOMICS 28

5 IDOLS OF WAR, SEX AND FATE 36

6 LORD OVER THE POWERS 43

7 LORD OF THE FUTURE 48

8 GUIDELINES FOR CONSCIENCE 57

9 'THE MRS HOUSDEN PRINCIPLE' 65

10 LORD OF OUR PERSECUTORS 73

11 DANIEL'S DREAM 81

12 CONFIDENT WITNESSES 88

13 GOD'S POWER FOR THE CHURCH 96

14 GOD'S GIFT AND OUR RESPONSE 108

15 SOMETHING TO SHOUT ABOUT 115

16 JESUS OUR JOY! 119

17 FIVE YEARS ON 125

FOREWORD

In this book, Professor Williamson fleshes out something of the biblical dimensions of what it means for a
Christian to confess Jesus is Lord. Written with a deft
touch and candid pastoral concern, this book will
deepen your grasp of what God has done for you in the
Lord Jesus Christ, and incite you to think through the
gospel afresh, and to respond to the Lord of the gospel
with joy and worship.

D. A. Carson

1
MUST WE BE NOBODY?

'The Lord is King; let the earth rejoice.' But we cannot rejoice if 'Jesus is Lord' means that we must lose our freedom, our choices, our identity almost. Some preachers seem to suggest that. Is that what the Bible says? Mercifully it is not.

Some years ago, during a service at our church, my eyes wandered to a banner that was propped up in the corner. It was to be part of a float that the children were preparing to enter in a local carnival, and on it was sewn in large cloth letters words based on Psalm 97:1: 'The Lord is king; let the earth rejoice.'

At the time, it seemed to me a very odd choice of text. My mind immediately went back to those many sermons through which I had sat so uncomfortably when the preacher would challenge us to consider whether Jesus was truly Lord of our lives. We called him our saviour and friend, but the New Testament repeatedly emphasizes that he is also Lord. So, is he Lord of *every part* of your life? And though I would slip down to sit as low as I could in my seat, the preacher's steely eyes always seemed to search me out as he thundered on: is he Lord of your bank balance? of your personal relationships? of your family life and of the way you carry on at work?

Well yes, I used to think, as far as possible he is; but then again there is always room for improvement, and so as the preacher went on to speak of 'those dark, hidden parts of your life, your thoughts, maybe, which you do not share with anyone else', I would admit to myself that I must pray about this and resolve to try harder in future. And so on to the closing hymn, when I would join fervently in singing something like, 'Take my life, and let it be consecrated, Lord, to thee'.

By a day or two later, however, precious little had changed. Outwardly reasonably successful and content, inside I was conscious of a growing sense of failure in my Christian life. Obviously, I was not all that I should be, and being looked to as a fairly respected member of the congregation only made me feel worse. All these thoughts, and more besides, flooded through my mind as I contemplated that text on the banner. 'The Lord is king; let the earth rejoice.' Why *should* the earth rejoice? In my experience, the idea of the Lord as king made me want to do anything but rejoice! Confess, pray, rededicate, yes; but rejoice? No, that was the last thing I felt like doing.

What made things worse was what I had been taught as a young student of theology by those who taught me the New Testament. We were told that probably the earliest Christian creed was the simple statement that 'Jesus is Lord'. Armed with this truth, those first Christians had gone out with such courage and joy that it could be said of them that they 'have turned the world upside down' (Acts 17:6, AV). Obviously for them their experience of the Lordship of Christ was vastly different from my own. I must be a very wayward Christian – that seemed to be the only conclusion to draw; and so it was back to square one again with more prayer and renewed resolve to do better in future.

LIVING WITH TENSION

Now it is only possible to live with that kind of tension between what one is taught and one's own experience for a certain length of time before something has to give (although I suspect that a great many Christians live with it for far longer than they should). As I continued to contemplate the text on the banner, I found myself thinking that really things could not go on like this. I had made every reasonable effort to put into practice what I had been taught, but to be honest it had not worked. I had been prepared to admit that the fault must be mine, but how long could this continue without the thought beginning to creep into my mind that perhaps it was not me, after all, that was so much at fault as the message I was being taught?

Though I was loath to admit it, the possibility had to be faced that this whole Christian message was fundamentally flawed, and that the New Testament could not after all be trusted. The gospel itself – the

9

message of God's full and free forgiveness for those who turn to him in faith — seemed fine, and I was fully prepared to argue with all-comers (as I frequently had) that Jesus had truly been raised from death and that Christianity therefore rested on a sound historical and intellectually respectable basis. But this business of the Lordship of Christ seemed to be like a vicious sting in the tail of the gospel that ruined the whole thing, robbing me of the joy and peace of mind that was promised at the start. The bottom line, then, was that Christianity as I was being taught it failed to deliver the goods, and perhaps the most honest course would be to chuck the whole thing over, regardless of the consequences. Unless . . .

Unless after all it was neither I nor the New Testament that was so wrong, but the preacher. Maybe, just maybe, he had not been telling us the whole story or had got it wrong somehow. After all, I remember once buying a radio and the man in the shop telling me the purpose of one of the buttons on it. Not being technically minded, I accepted his explanation without question, though it seemed a bit daft at the time. It was only years later when talking with a friend who knew all about these things that I realized that the salesman had no more clue about it than I. There was nothing wrong with the radio, nor with me as I tried to operate it as I had been instructed; it was the advice of the so-called expert that was at fault. Similarly, I was faced with the possibility that neither the New Testament nor I was at fault in this Christian business (due allowance made, of course, for my sinfulness and general shortcomings – but wasn't Christianity supposed to deal precisely with that problem?). Rather, those who were explaining it were themselves misleading me, not consciously or wilfully, I am sure, but nevertheless seriously off course.

BACK TO THE BIBLE

Clearly, if I was to save my Christian faith, to say nothing of my sanity, there was only one thing to be done, namely to read through the New Testament again specifically to see what it meant when it proclaimed so triumphantly that 'Jesus is Lord'. And as I did so, I discovered with growing excitement that the preacher had after all been mistaken. In this simple formula there was in fact a message which I had never heard, or at least properly understood, but which led me on to a sense of joy not previously experienced.

What follows in this little book is an account of what I discovered in those heady first days of reading the New Testament and of my subsequent reflections on it. I have preached on parts of this in a number of churches and once used it as the basis for a short series of talks on our local radio station. Always the message has been received with expressions of appreciation which makes me suspect that my experience is shared

11

by quite a number of sincere believers who are also struggling to bring their lives into closer conformity with the essential teaching of the Bible. So it has seemed worthwhile to share it with a wider circle by setting it out in print.

At the end some readers will doubtless shake their heads in astonishment that I had not grasped the point sooner; to them I would say, 'Then why didn't you tell me? How come you knew this truth but withheld it so that it is still not today the basis of all regular teaching in our churches?'

For others who are struggling with the kind of problems that I had, however, my prayer is that you too may be helped to see the whole thing in a new – or perhaps I should say an older – perspective.

Inevitably, we shall need to look closely at a number of passages in the Bible (I shall be using the New International Version throughout), and you may find it helpful to have the passages open in front of you as you read to check the various points for yourself. Nevertheless, I have tried to keep the discussion simple and straightforward. The books that I have written before have all been technical affairs on the Old Testament, meant largely for the small group of specialists or students with whom I regularly work. This book is not meant for them, however, at least not in their professional capacity, though if any of them should read it I hope that they will understand my reasons for this very different form of presentation. At the same time, I have naturally done my best to ensure that what I have written has beneath it a responsible attitude towards the various passages that we shall be looking at.

2

But death is the end, isn't it?

The first New Testament reference to the Lordship of Christ in the life of the church concerns death. The Jews crucified Jesus, but God made him 'Lord and Christ'. How can a dead man be Lord? Death is final.

According to the New Testament, the first occasion within the life of the church when the Lordship of Christ was proclaimed was at the end of Peter's speech on the Day of Pentecost. He explained that what had happened to the excited band of disciples gathered in an upper room was due to the impact of the coming of the Holy Spirit. He proclaimed that the Jesus who had so recently been crucified had been raised from death by God, and concluded: 'Therefore let all Israel be assured of this: God has made this Jesus, whom you crucified, both Lord and Christ' (Acts 2:36).

What did Peter mean? Going back over his words with this question in mind, we find that he first introduced Jesus in verses 22–24 with a brief outline of the main facts about his life, death and resurrection. This then leads him on to consider the effects of death in a little more detail. He quotes several verses from Psalm 16, which was believed to have been written by none other than King David. In the quotation, there is talk of

14

someone whose body would not 'see decay' in the grave after death (verse 27), something which was obviously not true of David himself. Even a casual visitor to Jerusalem would have had no difficulty in finding out where David had been buried and therefore where his memory was honoured. So it is with famous people from our own history whose tombs are often in prominent positions in the churches and cathedrals of our country.

WHAT HAPPENS AFTER DEATH?

Peter's reference to the facts of the death and burial of David would probably have stirred uneasy and even unhappy thoughts in the minds of his hearers. We do not know for certain what sort of hope they might have had concerning the possibility of life after death. In fact, they might not have even agreed amongst themselves on this matter. There was a wide variety of views on this subject in the ancient world generally and amongst the Jews in particular.

The Old Testament, which of course was their Bible, does not usually speculate much about what happens to a person at or after death. Most of the passages which say anything about this subject imply that death was effectively the end of a person's life as an individual. Without the idea which developed elsewhere of a person being made up of a body and a soul, it was almost inevitable that death should have been viewed as final. Indeed, one could see how the body decayed so that after a comparatively short time nothing was left but the bones, which might then be 'gathered to one's fathers' in a family tomb.

The passages which speak of Sheol as a place where some sort of shadowy life continues cannot be compared in any way with what we think of as life after death. After all, the dead cannot praise God there (cf. Psalms 6:5; 30:9; 88:10–12; 115:17; Isaiah 38:18–19). It was clearly a lifeless sort of life indeed! If there was any sense of an individual living on, it was in the idea that one's name lived on in that of one's children rather than in any personal sense.

This, at any rate, seems to have been the position of the Sadducees at the time of the New Testament. Because they accepted only the law of Moses (the first five books of the Old Testament) as authoritative, they refused to accept some of the speculations which developed amongst other groups. That was the basis for their attempt to ridicule Jesus with their question about a woman who had had several husbands in this life and what her marital status would be 'at the resurrection' (Mark 12:18–27). Indeed, the evangelist prefaces his account of this dispute with the explanation that the Sadducees 'say there is no resurrection'.

Similarly, there was a famous occasion when Paul was able to throw his opposition (consisting of both Sadducees and Pharisees) into confusion by remarking that it was 'because of my hope in the resurrection of the dead' that he was being called to account (Acts 23:6–10).

This would probably have been a minority opinion among those who first heard Peter preach, however. The majority would have sided rather with the Pharisees. They took more seriously than the Sadducees the hints in some of the later books of the Old Testament, hints which were developed further in the period between the Old and New Testaments, that death could not be the final end.

A number of factors may have contributed to this development. They saw that God's justice is not always worked out on this earth, so that perhaps it was only in some form of an after-life that wrong was put right and the wicked punished. This makes sense at the time when the Jews began to suffer religious persecution at the hands of foreign rulers. How else could faith in God's promises to his people be maintained?

However, this developing belief was not a Christian view of resurrection or life after death. Daniel 12:2, for instance, appeared to say that only the extremely righteous or the extremely wicked would rise to receive their just deserts. Nothing would necessarily be changed so far as the majority of ordinary people were concerned. Furthermore, it seems quite likely that, when the later Jewish rabbis speak of a life 'in the age to come', they are talking about life in a future age on this earth, not the 'eternal life' which we are accustomed to think of. So even in these more developed views, there was little by way of personal comfort to be found in the idea of resurrection as then held.

Still others, of course (always assuming that they had given the matter any serious thought), might have been more influenced by the concepts of the Greek world. Those Jews who lived outside the land of Palestine would have come into regular contact with it. But nobody on his death-bed would thank a preacher for trying to minister solace on the basis of Greek descriptions of the underworld as we know of them from the works of mythology that have been preserved for us.

PERHAPS DEATH IS THE END?

It thus seems that the brute fact of death posed an uncomfortable and uncomforting problem for those who listened to Peter preaching. When Paul writes of death as 'the last enemy' that must be destroyed (1 Corinthians 15:26), he is not using empty words. In the environment in which he was brought up, Death could be spelled with a capital 'D' – a sinister and malevolent power which seemed almost to take on a personal character as it stalked and eventually over-whelmed each individual.

It seems to me, however, that in this regard many of us today have not progressed much further than they. Indeed, our materialistic world-view, which regards life in wholly and exclusively scientific terms, means that people see death as the end. By definition, any talk of life beyond the physical world which we know is automatically excluded. Indeed, this point of view is precisely what led to the development of the existentialism so popular a couple of decades ago which took almost as its starting point the assertion that death obliges us to regard this life itself as absurd – pointless and without purpose. Virtually any response could then be justified, whether good or ill. There was no moral ground on which to base decisions that affected the way one lived except the doubtful one that we should be 'true to ourselves'.

Few ordinary people, however, have the desire to press the logic of their beliefs to the extremes of the philosophers (even though the philosophers were in fact doing us a service in showing us where so much current thinking must inevitably lead). Rather, we have become adept at masking the truth from ourselves and pretending that it will go away if we do not look at it. This, of course, has led to a fund of absurdities and funny stories which serve only to highlight the point.

There is a story told about Handley Moule, a bishop of Durham in the early years of this century, for instance. Though I cannot vouch for the truth of this, it is said that one day when he visited his doctor he was told that he was seriously ill and that he should go to Switzerland for a complete rest to aid his recovery. The bishop protested that he was far too busy with the work of his diocese; he couldn't possibly think of going. 'Well,' the doctor said, 'it's either Switzerland or Heaven.' 'Oh,' replied the Bishop, 'well, if it's as bad as that, I'd better go to Switzerland!'

Again, in his book *The Jesus Hope* (Hemel Hempstead, 1974, p. 69), Steven Travis recounts, 'A minister was visiting a man who was very ill. At the foot of the stairs the sick man's wife whispered apprehensively, "Say something *hopeful* to him, won't you? – not about heaven and all that" '!

3

JESUS' DEATH: THE BEGINNING

The apostle Peter claimed that Jesus was Lord even over King Death. Leave aside, for the moment, whether Jesus is Lord over us – he is Lord over our worst enemy! This does not limit our freedom. It extends it into eternity.

No doubt we could all tell such stories as the ones at the end of the last chapter. They are not to be taken too seriously. They do not reveal what we really think. Or do they? Perhaps the very fact that we all catch ourselves talking like this on occasions shows us that we have unconsciously absorbed the ethos of our age, which is to hold the subject of death at arm's length.

AVOIDING THE ISSUE

Death is not considered a polite subject for conversation, and even when its reality presses in upon us, as it must do from time to time through the death of a relative or friend, we use all kinds of language to cushion ourselves from the truth. People no longer die, but merely 'pass away'; they are laid in caskets in a chapel of rest rather than in coffins in a mortuary; their corpses are not buried but their 'mortal remains are laid to rest,' and so on.

More seriously, we often refuse to face the fact that

someone we love may be terminally ill. This makes the whole process of dying even more painful for ourselves (to say nothing of the one who is sick) than it already is. Admittedly, recent years have seen a shift in these attitudes because of the remarkable and courageous work of those who have established hospices for the dying which minister to patient and family alike. But I suspect it will be many long years before there is any significant change in the way western society confronts these matters as a whole.

The astonishing popularity of spiritism and related activities at all levels of society may be linked to this refusal to come to terms with the fact of death. The diabolical offer of the possibility of contact with those who have 'passed over' hinders the bereaved from coming to terms with their loss. The form of survival which it presupposes for those who have died can do nothing to help those still alive to face the fact of their own mortality with anything other than gloom.

I have touched on only one or two of the ways in which death is treated in the modern world. You could no doubt add your own. But perhaps this is enough to suggest that we may be in a similar situation to those who first listened to Peter's Pentecost sermon. Only the packaging has changed; underneath, we should have no difficulty in identifying ourselves with them in their confusion and even dread of the approach of King Death.

LOVE STRONGER THAN DEATH

What, then, did Peter say that could possibly have brought a change to this depressing scene? There seem to me to be two things.

First, the proclamation that Jesus has been made Lord in this context implies in particular that he is Lord especially over King Death. Jesus had entered the realm of death, and he had been buried in a tomb like David and thousands of others like him before. But that was not the end of the story. God had raised Jesus from death into a new sphere of life. Of that, Peter and his fellow disciples were quite certain because they had met him, and they were not in the least afraid or ashamed to be witnesses to the fact. 'That . . . which we have heard, which we have seen with our eyes . . . and our hands have touched – this we proclaim concerning the Word of life' (1 John 1:1).

So when Peter declared that Jesus had been made Lord, he was claiming that Jesus is Lord in an ultimate sense – that he had been shown to be stronger than one of the strongest powers around, death itself. His resurrection had demonstrated that death had met its match and been defeated; it had not been able to hold on to this one whom it thought that it had claimed like everyone else.

But secondly, and equally important, this new and greater Lord is none other than Jesus of Nazareth, the one of whom Peter said earlier that he was 'a man accredited by God to you by miracles, wonders and signs, which God did among you through him, as you yourselves know' (Acts 2:22). That was surely the most startling point. The one who is now Lord is the one whom many of his listeners had known, and whose ministry they had followed: the one who had been prepared to touch the untouchable leper; the one who had restored human dignity to the frightened and lonely woman whose twelve-year haemorrhage had meant that she was driven apart from normal contact with society; the one who even at the end of a tiring day had not been too preoccupied with his own exhaustion to take the children in his arms and bless them; and the one who, besides much else, had found the strength and the love to pray for forgiveness for his cruel and hardened executioners.

Now if this approachable Jesus had been made a Lord stronger than death, then that cast the whole business of the end of life into a wholly new context. For on the one hand, to entrust one's eternal destiny into his keeping was to be enfolded in a love that was truly stronger than death. He had proved his power in this sphere; his credentials were impeccable! 'No-one can snatch them out of my hand' (John 10:28) is no empty boast, but guaranteed by the fact that he is Lord over the strongest malevolent power which might try to do just that. To be in his care would be to find oneself in the place of greatest safety.

But on the other hand, to take that step of self-entrusting would be for Peter's audience no step in the dark, no blind leap of faith hoping against hope. Rather, it would be to move into the shelter of one whom they already knew, and who had demonstrated in his life that he always had time for any who came to him in real need. As he himself had said in summary of his whole attitude and outlook, 'Come to me, all you who are weary and burdened, and I will give you rest' (Matthew 11:28).

No wonder the disciples were so overjoyed on that day of Pentecost that they were at first thought to be drunk! The Lordship of Christ was now for them the very ground of their assurance for life and for death. Jesus, the Jesus whom they had come to know, trust, respect and even love – this Jesus was now seen to be Lord after all, and not King Death, who they thought had dealt the final blow to all the hopes raised during those brief years of their following him around Judea and Galilee.

WHAT DOES THIS MEAN FOR US?

Two important consequences follow from this. First, we can see that the emphasis is not, as I had always thought, on the issue of whether Jesus has full authority over every aspect of my own individual life. Peter does not seem to have touched on that aspect at all. Rather, the emphasis is on the proclamation that *Jesus*, not death, is Lord. If I can put it this way, I had been saying the phrase with a stress on the last word –

'Jesus is *Lord*'; in other words, he is not just saviour or redeemer, but also Lord, and hence the next question was always, 'Is he *your* Lord?' But it now seems that Peter would have put the emphasis on the first word of the phrase: '*Jesus* (and not Death) is Lord'.

It may seem a very slight change in the way we say it, but it makes a world of difference to the meaning! Instead of being a heavy, depressing, almost threatening statement, it is suddenly transformed into the most wonderful good news that one could possibly imagine, full of comfort and reassurance: 'Since the children have flesh and blood, he too shared in their humanity so that by his death he might destroy him who holds the power of death – that is, the devil – and free those who all their lives were held in slavery by their fear of death' (Hebrews 2:14–15).

Secondly, we can see that the proclamation that Jesus is Lord was first made in the context of some other threatening powers which the listeners might have at first presumed was the real Lord, in this case, death. It is in the face of that other threat that the realization that Jesus is Lord comes to be such a liberating message.

I went on to look at the other places where the same formula is used, asking myself now whether there was in those passages too some other potential threat over which the Lordship of Jesus might similarly be a source of relief and encouragement. There was! In fact, it seemed to be true of every occurrence of the phrase in the New Testament. Hence my mounting sense of wonder as I realized that this was a common thread that linked all these passages together and which simply made the depth and the expanse of that simple little phrase more and more wonderful.

So let's move on to the next passage, not now following the order of the New Testament itself, but beginning to group the passages by common subject matter. Just as death was a mute and external threat to the peace of mind of those first-century readers, so too were the 'dumb idols' of which Paul speaks in his first letter to the church in Corinth.

4

THE IDOL OF GLOBAL ECONOMICS

*We no longer believe in the power of idols but all our
lives are affected, even dominated, by forces we can do
nothing about. The power of worldwide supply and
demand seems to have a sinister and blind life of its own
and is rapidly spinning us out of control.*

When I first came across the use of the expression
'Jesus is Lord' in 1 Corinthians 12:3, I was puzzled. It
comes, after all, in what is a decidedly peculiar
sentence: 'Therefore I tell you that no-one who is
speaking by the Spirit of God says, "Jesus be cursed,"
and no-one can say, "Jesus is Lord," except by the
Holy Spirit.' However, I applied my self-imposed rule
of looking around in the context to see whether there
was anything that would help explain it. Sure enough
I saw that in the previous sentence there was again a
description of a rival claim to lordship over people's
lives, this time 'dumb [mute] idols' (AV).

In the western world at the end of the twentieth
century, it is hard for us to enter into the way idol
worshippers thought in the first-century Roman
empire. Most of us brought up within the heritage of
the Jewish and Christian tradition completely repudi-
ate such an approach to the supernatural. We have

absorbed the atmosphere of the sarcastic satire of Isaiah 44:9–20, where the prophet mocks at the folly of those who build idols. It still brings a wry smile to our lips as we read of the man who makes an image out of part of a tree as an object of worship, even though he has made it himself, and who does not see the nonsense of taking the bits and pieces that are left over to make a fire by which he can cook and keep himself warm. It is all so patently ridiculous that we are apt to dismiss the whole undertaking as beneath contempt.

THE IDOLATER'S VIEWPOINT

Effective as such satire may be it makes no attempt, of course, to see the situation from the point of view of the idol worshipper himself. He might have replied that of course he did not think that the image was itself a god. Rather, it was a *representation* of the god, who was in some sense a spirit. It was a focus for his worship and devotion rather than the object of worship itself.

Perhaps we can see this from the attitude many of us have towards a church building. Although we know that God is not contained in a particular building and that we can meet with God at any time and in any place, we nevertheless still often refer to a church as 'the house of God'. We are still apt to drop our voices and behave quietly when we go inside. A friend told me that quite often when he goes early into our church to get things ready for a service he calls out a cheery 'Good morning, God!' We still seem to need a focus both in time and space for our particular acts of service and worship.

The difference between us and idol worshippers, then, has more to do with the character of the God with whom we have to deal. As the early Christian church began to spread beyond the narrow confines of its original Jewish cradle, it had to come to terms with the widespread paganism of the time. Even writing to Christians, John still needed to exhort his readers to 'keep yourselves from idols' (1 John 5:21), while Paul too had to urge the Corinthian believers to 'flee from idolatry' (1 Corinthians 10:14).

In the passage from which we started out in this chapter, Paul shows us more about the nature of idols. He reminds the Corinthians that before they had become Christians they had first been 'influenced' and then been 'led astray' to what he calls 'these dumb idols' (1 Corinthians 12:2, AV). And that, it seems to me, sums up the real problem for the dedicated idol worshipper. Idols cannot explain where they are taking you, and even if they could their answers wouldn't be worth much because they are fundamentally irrational. You never knew quite which way they were going to jump, so to speak. No matter what offerings you brought, they could be smiling one day only to become implacably opposing forces for ill the next. The reason is obvious. The idol was not concerned for the well-being of its devotees. They were there primarily to satisfy the desires of the idol, and since its desires were apparently whimsical, one could never be sure of having done the right thing by it, or of not having offended its changing feelings.

Now all this seems to be – and is – a world apart from 'the God and Father of our Lord Jesus Christ' (2 Corinthians 1:2). But that does not mean to say that we are immune from the impact of latter-day dumb idols, even if the way we treat them is vastly different. Still today our lives are subject to a whole range of voiceless and irrational forces. They too seem benign one day and terrifying the next and in either case quite beyond our control. Let's consider a few examples.

ECONOMIC FORCES

A great deal about the way that we live is determined by the amount of money we have. But how much control are we able to exercise over our income? Most of us are employed or else dependent on someone else who is employed. Immediately, then, we are not directly in a position to change what our wage-packet or salary will be. Of course, there are trade unions to look after our interests, to try to improve working conditions and ensure that we receive a fair return for our work, but even they cannot draw increased wages out of a hat. Protest as they may, they cannot stop a factory or business closing down if the goods or services on offer are no longer in demand. So, when some politician announces that because of a downturn in world trade so many thousand people are likely to lose their jobs, I can't help remembering Harold Wilson's famous remark that, for somebody without a job, unemployment is 100%.

'Out there', there are pressures of global proportions which we cannot understand, explain or influence. And it is really no easier for employers or management. They in turn cannot do anything to change such factors as market forces, interest rates, government regulations and the many other problems with which they have to contend.

So who does control these matters? You might suppose that it is the government, but if you listen carefully to what our leading treasury officials say, you will soon realize that their room for manoeuvre is also heavily restricted. On the one hand, they too are hemmed in by what is going on in the wider world, and much of their legislation is more a response to that than an attempt to influence it. On the other hand, the measures that they take are inevitably extremely crude and often fall far more heavily on some trapped individuals than others.

Let me give a personal example. We were trying to sell our house in a highly desirable area; there should have been no difficulty. But just before we put the house on the market the laws concerning mortgages were changed, while at the same time interest rates shot up. The result was dramatic, even if it could not have been predicted as little as a few weeks before: the bottom simply dropped out of the market and we were left thousands of pounds worse off. Now who intended that to happen? We certainly didn't, and I do not believe that the government did either. Their aim was simply to trim the economy by a small amount because of other external pressures, but of course they could not spread that small amount evenly across the board. So there really is no simple answer to the question 'whose fault was it?', even though its impact on us individually was dramatic.

GLOBAL FORCES

Perhaps you think, however, that my example is too selfish. After all, what proportion of the world's population even has a house to sell in the first place? We have been made acutely aware in recent years of the grinding poverty that afflicts so many countries on our planet. Given the present international set-up it is most unlikely that anything realistic is going to be done about it. We are talking about a world population that is made up of individuals who day after day are forced to live out the miserable consequences of what has happened.

The essential problem can be simply stated. A developing country needs money to improve its situation. Lacking rich natural resources, it turns to the major western banks and similar institutions for a loan. On that loan it has to pay heavy interest, which further burdens the people who are least in a position to sustain it. And why? – in order further to enrich those who are already rich enough to be in a position to be able to make the loan in the first place.

Now, it is not my purpose here to point to possible solutions to this problem, nor to point out its all too obvious injustices. Rather, I want you to consider how it appears to a peasant farmer or city small-trader in a country affected by this situation. What realistic possibility is there of him or her breaking out of such a poverty trap? Occasionally, we hear or read of some exceptional individual with the determination, initiative, and – let's be honest – good fortune making it from rags to riches. But for every one such there must be at least a million who do not, and indeed who could not. Nearly all those in this situation must inevitably remain there. They must draw the strong fatalistic conclusion not only that they do not control their destiny but that there is no such personal control at all.

So, the conclusion seems inescapable: at least one important aspect of our lives is in the hands of impersonal forces which are unpredictable and apparently irrational. It is not that we need to imagine some supreme demon maliciously pulling the puppet strings to which we must all dance; I have no doubt that much of what I have been talking about could be attributed by economic analysts to the converging decisions of thousands, if not millions, of individual people. But their collective decision-making builds up into powers that go far beyond their own, and thus by extension, far beyond the powers of anyone else.

So we become mere cogs in the economic wheel, numbers on a payroll, statistics in bureaucracy's account books. I am all in favour of the freedom of the individual, but it means nothing at all until we come to terms with the fact that it is very limited.

5

IDOLS OF WAR, SEX AND FATE

We are at the mercy of conflicts we do not want, desires that overwhelm our reason and the terror of the unknown. Is it surprising that many turn to superstition to try to foresee and control the uncontrollable?

INTERNATIONAL FORCES

Another powerful influence which affects all our lives is the realm of international politics. The most dramatic example has to be that of war. Now I happen to be fortunate enough to have been born an Englishman a couple of years after the conclusion of the Second World War, and so I have not had the personal experience that many of you have had, and as undoubtedly millions alive today in other parts of the world have had, and sadly continue to have.

Even so, I vividly remember one trivial example of the effects of war. As a young boy, I grew up in London with rationing still in force. One day, my mother took me to a large hall where, she told me, we were going to collect our ration coupons for sweets for the last time. I was devastated.

As we were given those precious slips of paper that had been such an important part of my 'economy', I mused on what life would be like without them. Once they had gone, I thought, I would never taste sweets again! It was some while before it was explained to a very miserable young lad that in future he would be allowed to buy as many sweets as his pocket money could afford!

NATIONS OUT OF CONTROL

But what of those of my parents' generation who watched the events of the 1930s developing with what must have seemed like an inexorable inevitability towards the tragic outbreak of war in 1939? How much control could they exercise over the progress of events that would profoundly affect the lives of every man, woman and child in the kingdom? None at all. And subsequently, could not the same be said of the populations of Vietnam, Afghanistan, Central America, Angola, Iran, Iraq and oh! so many other theatres of war in the decades between?

We may sometimes blame a single individual for a war, but those individuals could never have dragged their followers into war unaided. Historians today are far more concerned to analyse the general social and economic conditions and forces which allow such an individual to emerge on the world stage in the first place. The causes of war are far more complex than war films and comic book heroes might lead us to expect – so complex, in fact, that we seem quickly to be coming full circle again to those impersonal forces, or 'dumb idols', from which we started out.

PERSONAL FORCES

So far I have concentrated on forces outside of ourselves which have a profound influence on us, but we have very little control over them. There is, however, another direction from which such unwelcome forces come at us, and that is from within. All of us possess a package of emotions, instincts and driving forces which can be either beneficial or harmful, and which most of the time we manage to keep under more or less tight control. But sometimes they sneak out and then surprise or even appal us with their intensity or ferocity.

Self-preservation

The destructive effects of these human driving forces are all too apparent in modern society, but only the outward expression of them has changed. I do not think society is getting either progressively worse or better when it comes to human behaviour.

I am told that the strongest of these natural instincts is the drive for self-preservation. Of course that has a healthy and necessary side to it; without it we should be immune to danger and careless of any threat to ourselves or our families.

The negative side of the coin, however, is that, because of the way in which our characters have been perverted by sin, our own drive for self-preservation becomes twisted into an aggressive attitude towards others, and not only when we are threatened. Thus loss of temper and irrational violence well up inside us all from time to time. Most of us manage to control it for most of the time, but we cannot hide this ugly side of our nature from ourselves even if we hide it from others. Have you never caught yourself expressing disapproval over some violent incident described on the breakfast-time news only then to become equally aggressive towards other road-users? It is extraordinary how tenaciously most of us defend every inch of our 'territory' on the motorway when caught up in a traffic jam and how aggressively we respond to those who seem to infringe it to their own 'unfair' advantage.

Sex

Perhaps the second most powerful of our human driving forces is related to sex. Again, there is a God-given purpose behind this, for without it the human race would have ceased to survive long since! But need I emphasize the negative side? Perhaps it is enough to observe, as a friend of mine is fond of doing in his sermons, that every time I point a finger at someone else, there are inevitably three fingers pointing back at me. We can easily get all sanctimonious and pious in condemning the permissive society, but we might do better first to bear in mind the story Jesus told about someone who offered to remove the speck of dust from his brother's eye without first taking care of the whacking great plank sticking out of his own (Matthew 7:3–5).

In calmer or more reflective moments, we perhaps are prepared to allow that none of us is immune from these strong inward pressures. My point here is not to condemn or criticize (who am I, after all, to do so?), nor even to make you feel guilty; we all have problems enough with guilt without my adding to them. Rather, my point is simply to underline that once again we are not so much the masters of our own destiny as we might like to think. Our freedom is very limited, both from within and without, and it is easy to understand those Christians at Corinth to whom Paul wrote about 'dumb idols' by whom they had been influenced and led astray.

RELIGIOUS FORCES

There is one more angle from which pressure comes but which we are powerless to control, and that is religion, understood in its widest sense. At this point I am not thinking about a truly biblical Christianity, though sadly even some versions of that have been twisted by some into a force to control others. Rather, I have in mind the attitude which seems to be surprisingly widely held today that our lives are controlled by some power 'out there' to which our best response is a fatalistic acceptance of the situation.

Your future in the stars?
The most obvious example of this is the whole business of reading the stars and trying to gain some

guidance for life from them. Many normally sensible people are quite convinced that the time of year when they were born has influenced how they will relate to others. Many, of course, take this a great deal further and so read daily or weekly in the popular press what is 'in the stars' for them in the near future. In company, we laugh at such ideas and try to pretend that it is nothing more than a harmless bit of fun – a joke that nobody really believes in. But the popularity of horoscopes has demanded that they even get prominence on television breakfast-time programmes, alongside otherwise serious and rational news and other items.

Some while ago, our local radio station regularly included a slot for one such 'expert' on a popular morning show. We live in a society which generally believes that things have natural causes and effects, and that, given enough knowledge, a scientific explanation could be provided for all that happens. Very many people, however, nurture the secret belief that really it is not so; somewhere out there are other puppet-masters who are pulling the strings.

I will not dwell here upon the irony, to say nothing of the absurdity, of this situation. In a sophisticated, twentieth-century society, we come as close as we possibly can to what Paul had in mind when he wrote of dumb idols so long ago. They are irrational – you cannot yourself predict how the situation will develop from day to day. And yet, they are all powerful – they determine vast acres of experience, and the best you can hope to do is take steps to avoid the dangers they present or cash in on the opportunities they are supposed to offer. Moreover, they have their own high priests, experts who are initiated into the secret workings of the universe and upon whose direction you are forced to rely.

I do not imply that everyone reading this book is a fatalist, though I think that it is very helpful as an illustration of the way in which we can be trapped into opting out of control of, and hence responsibility for, our lives and actions. It underlines the consequences of many of those attitudes which we were looking at earlier in this chapter. But even if we do not subscribe to this particular brand of nonsense, many of us do have a sense of some unknown destiny hanging over our lives. Superstition is still very much alive and well, and I don't just mean not walking under ladders. In fact, what seemed to be one of those parts of the New Testament most removed from our modern experience turns out to be one with which all of us can identify most readily. The dumb idols of economic, international, personal and fatalistic forces are little changed from the idols of the first century; it is just that now they are masquerading under different, more modern and so supposedly more palatable, names.

6

LORD OVER THE POWERS

The situation looks bleak. But turn back to the Jesus we meet in the New Testament. God created the world through him and later raised him from his tomb. Jesus is reliable, he is loving and he is Lord over all this apparently uncontrollable chaos. That is no threat to us – it's a relief.

The situation seems bleak indeed. I have only given a few examples, and many of you will have experiences of your own screaming out at you for inclusion in the list. But clearly, that is not the end of the story!

Alongside his reference to the dumb idols, Paul also tells his readers that 'no-one can say, "Jesus is Lord", except by the Holy Spirit' (1 Corinthians 12:3). Perhaps now we can begin to appreciate something of the radical alternative, the new world-view, which he is offering us here. Contrasted with the irrational forces we have been thinking about, there is another force, a different Lord – and that Lord is none other than Jesus himself. As in our first example, relating to King Death, two points need to be emphasized here.

CREATOR OF LIFE: RISEN FROM DEATH

The first point is that Jesus is a superior power to any other that I have mentioned. Paul and the other New

Testament writers stress the extraordinary fact that it was through Jesus that God created the world and all that is in it. Even if there are situations and problems beyond our control which seem to be overwhelming, they are nevertheless vastly inferior to him, as inferior, in fact, as the model is to the one who made it. But what is more, his superiority has been shown by those events which are central to our faith.

In exposing himself to death, it was as though he was putting himself at the mercy (ironic phrase!) of all those political, subhuman and demonic powers which we experience in milder forms in our own lives. The sealed tomb seemed to portray their ultimate triumph. Even Jesus, they thought, was not immune from their influence; at its very centre, the universe is controlled by these impersonal and ultimately malevolent forces.

But what is this? 'The third day, he rose again from the dead, he ascended into Heaven, and is seated at the right hand of God the Father Almighty!' So countless Christians have affirmed in the Creed week by week, perhaps not always grasping the momentous implications of what they have been saying. Paul puts it more graphically in Colossians 2:15: 'And having disarmed the powers and authorities, he made a public spectacle of them, triumphing over them by the cross.' Again, in his Revelation, John is given a glimpse into heaven, and what is the first thing he sees there? 'At once I was in the Spirit, and there before me was a throne in heaven with someone sitting on it'

(Revelation 4:2). Yes! The tomb was empty, but now at the heart of the universe was seen a throne, speaking of government, and moreover, someone was sitting on that throne, so that the world's future is in the hands of a rational being. Revelation goes on to talk of some terrifying events that would leave us all speechless with horror were we not first told that God is in charge. They are controlled by a rational God for the ultimate destruction of evil and the vindication of faith and righteousness. And as you will remember, John's vision does not stop there, for in the next chapter another is seen to be on that same throne, 'a Lamb, looking as if it had been slain' (5:6), so that this future world government will also be controlled by principles of love and mercy alongside justice and judgment.

HE IS LOVING: HE IS RELIABLE

This brings me to the second point we need to remember from Paul's affirmation that 'Jesus is Lord'. Not only is Jesus superior in power to the dumb idols, but his power is of a different order, all summed up in the use of the name of his humanity – Jesus. His purposes towards mankind were wholly and single-mindedly for good. No irrational being here, unpredictable and menacing, but rather one who in the face of every situation could find it in his heart to act only in love. You know where you are with such a person.

Foreseeing danger, he may have to correct or redirect our paths, and at the time this may seem

45

puzzling if not positively painful, but the one thing we can be sure of is that it is not irrational. To have entrusted one's life into the keeping of this Lord is to pass into the care and protection of one who we know from the manner of his life and bearing was all love, all concern for the ultimate well-being of others. To know that Jesus, and not some dumb idol, is Lord is to be set free from anxiety about the future course of events. We are assured that our lives are governed by a concerned and rational Person who works all the circumstances of even our workaday lives together for our eventual good (Romans 8:28). Once again, it is the Jesus whose attractive personality we know from the gospel story who is also now Lord in contrast to the deadening and desolating influence of any dumb idol.

To grasp this truth, I suggest, is to turn our whole attitude around. It may still be true that we do not control the political life or the economy of our planet, but that does not mean that they control us either. They can safely be left in the hands of one who is stronger than all, leaving us free to develop our characters in relationship with him and with one another, finding his glory even in the ordinary where previously it was veiled from our sight.

Given the choice, which would you rather have as Lord – the dumb idols or Jesus? Put like that, there seems to be no choice at all. Yet many still fail to see the possibility of escape which the teaching of the real

Lordship of Christ affords. However, we are not through yet with the forces that are ranged against our lives, even if the next group we must consider are considerably more garrulous than idols.

7

LORD OF THE FUTURE

The only certainty about our future is physical death for everyone. This is small comfort. But Jesus also went through death – and came out the other side. He is Lord of the future as well as the present and so we can have confidence in our own future.

There is a well-known Chinese proverb which says that 'prediction is a difficult business, especially predicting the future'! No matter how perceptive or clear-sighted we may be, we can never have absolute confidence in the prediction even of so-called experts, let alone the rest of us. At the end of 1989 Communist governments fell like a row of dominoes in Eastern Europe, but I do not remember anyone foretelling that extraordinary chain of events. Furthermore, who would dare say what the political map of Europe will look like by the time you may happen to be reading these lines?

I remember a colleague of mine, who lectures on modern China, being interviewed on the radio at the time when students and others were demonstrating for greater democracy in Beijing. The ghastly events of a few days afterwards proved that even with all his knowledge of modern China he could not see how the regime there would react.

We could all produce examples of the same sort of thing closer to home. If it were not so, the gambling business would not be so keen to invite us to lay our bets on sporting events, the outcome of general elections and goodness knows what else besides. Nor would so many people resort to the occult in a vain and dangerous attempt to know the unknowable.

WHAT WILL THE FUTURE HOLD?

The unorthodox writer of the book of Ecclesiastes in the Old Testament was well aware of the uncertainties of life. 'For who knows what is good for a man in life, during the few and meaningless days he passes through like a shadow? Who can tell him what will happen under the sun after he is gone?' (6:12). Sometimes, an unforeseen turn of events can make a mockery of someone's efforts to amass riches: 'I have seen a grievous evil under the sun: wealth hoarded to the harm of its owner, or wealth lost through some misfortune, so that when he has a son there is nothing left for him' (5:13–14), for after all 'time and chance happen to them all' (9:11). One thing is certain, however, and that is that we shall all end up in the grave. This rather gloomy reflection gets repeated time and time again throughout Ecclesiastes. It serves to put all our efforts in this life under a distinct shadow.

Doubts about the future, together with its certain end, so far as we as individuals are concerned, pick up the themes which we looked at in the previous chapters. Death on the one hand, and uncontrollable pressures on our lives on the other, mean that we do not know what is going to happen to us. The forces which determine these things are too varied and too strong for us to be able to understand or to regulate.

For most people for most of the time, this is not the source of any great anxiety. After all, how dull life would be if on waking up each morning we knew exactly what was going to happen to us that day! It would leave us feeling, quite rightly, that we had no wills of our own. We should have become mere robots, acting out the script of some divinely-written drama in which the actors themselves were of no importance whatever. No, the very uncertainties of life are what make us responsible as human beings. The fact that we can exercise choice means that we matter as people. It is not a freedom that we should lightly surrender.

On the other hand what parent has not spent anxious nights worrying about how their child will 'turn out'? What businessman has never worried about how a particular deal will end? 'It's the waiting that's the worst part,' we say, as we anticipate the outcome of some examination or medical report or news of a relative who is in danger. For some, anxieties of this kind can have a crippling effect, because they are unwilling to face the possible consequences of their own decisions.

Others worry profoundly about the course our planet seems to be taking. For some it is the prospect of global conflict involving the kind of weapons that are now available to the superpowers, and perhaps what is worse, their spread to other smaller and less responsible nations or even terrorist groups; for others, it is the ecological crisis which, on current predictions, could mean that there will be no habitable planet to bequeath to our children or grandchildren. For others again, it is the ugly head of religious fanaticism and bigotry which seems increasingly to be controlling world affairs. These are major matters, and I should emphasize that nothing I say in this chapter is meant to diminish the threat which they pose. I do not suggest that Christians are smugly immune from them, nor that they should not be playing a full part in getting rid of them.

Nevertheless, I have just spoken of these issues as a 'threat', and that brings us back to the major issue. Is the future another force concerning which the Lordship of Jesus may have something more positive to say? The answer is an emphatic 'Yes!', as I quickly realized when my hunt through the New Testament for passages proclaiming that 'Jesus is Lord' brought me to Philippians 2.

'EVERY KNEE WILL BOW'

In Philippians chapter 2 Paul is encouraging his readers to be humble in their dealings with one another. 'Each of you should look not only to your own interests,' he says, 'but also to the interests of others' (verse 4). He reminds them of the example which Jesus himself had set. In doing so, we are told by scholars of the New Testament, he quotes from an early Christian hymn. Still today, preachers will often quote lines from a familiar hymn to give added weight to what they are saying, and there seems to be no reason why Paul should not have done the same. (Incidentally, people often forget the main purpose that Paul had in mind when they read for devotional purposes the famous verses which follow!)

This hymn (verses 6–11) falls into two main parts and, strictly speaking, it is only the first half which illustrates the point that Paul is making. It tells how, despite the exalted position which Christ enjoyed, he did not think of hanging on to it. He had regard also for the interests of others, and he 'made himself nothing', or 'emptied himself' (RSV), and took the form, not just of a man, but of a servant. Nor did he stop there – he further humbled himself by becoming 'obedient to death – even death on a cross'. It is difficult to think of a more humbling and yet powerful illustration of the attitude which we proud and selfish Christians should adopt.

But Paul, even though he has made his point, rushes on in his excitement to remind us that because of Christ's obedience at such cost, 'God exalted him to the highest place'. We, of course, naturally think first of the resurrection and Christ's triumphant return to glory, but in fact the hymn puts it rather differently: God 'gave him the name that is above every name'. What is this name, and why is it so important?

Many people think that it is the name 'Jesus', because the passage goes on immediately to say that 'at the name of Jesus every knee should bow'. However, he already had that name at the time of his humiliation, and what's more there were many other Jews who were also called Jesus. It looks as though we have only reached a 'staging post' on the journey of Christ's exaltation, and that we should read on.

As we do so, we come to the climax of the passage with the words 'and [that] every tongue [should] confess that Jesus Christ is Lord' (verse 11). Here indeed is a new name for Jesus Christ – that of Lord. It seems that there is a deliberate reference here back to the words of God himself in Isaiah 42:8, 'I am the LORD; that is my name! I will not give my glory to another'; and 45:23, 'By myself I have sworn . . . [that] before me every knee will bow; by me every tongue will swear.'

In other words, God is now going to share with the obedient Jesus his holy and personal name which previously had been jealously reserved for himself. This, then, is certainly a new name, and it indicates that from now on Jesus will share in God's power and authority, an authority which includes the right to control the future just as much as he has the past (see, for instance, Isaiah 41:4; 42:9; 43:18–19; 45:21).

The future, of course, is very much in mind in our passage in Philippians 2. The time is coming when everyone will bow at the name of Jesus, and when everyone will acknowledge that he is Lord. Everyone? Yes! But not just every*one*. Included also in this universal acclamation will be all 'in heaven and on earth and under the earth' (verse 10), which looks like a pretty comprehensive description of every kind of power, whether we choose to call it human, sub-human, demonic, impersonal or whatever. Indeed, we can reasonably say that it also includes all those forces which we thought about earlier.

JESUS IS LORD OF THE FUTURE

Now for some, it seems clear, this worship of the Lord Jesus Christ will be a matter of compulsion. They will finally be obliged to admit that their rejection of Jesus had been mistaken and wrong-headed. But for the Christian? Surely the occasion will be one for a joyful and grateful personal encounter with the living saviour. By his death he has accomplished so much both for the individual and for all redeemed humanity. Words cannot express what that day will be like, for 'now we see but a poor reflection as in a mirror; then we shall see face to face. Now I know in part; then I shall know fully' (1 Corinthians 13:12).

For a Christian, the future is ultimately not a journey into the unknown, but rather a movement towards a meeting with the Lord. He holds the final destiny of the world in his own hands, but (and this is the main point) he is already known as the Jesus of history and of the present. The progression in the hymn from the person of Jesus to the exalted Lord of the future is no accident. It reflects our own past, present and future.

We have learned who Jesus is from his life of service and self-sacrifice here on earth. It was the kind of life which draws and attracts, which does not turn away or bludgeon its way to power. It was a life laid down in order that we might receive life, a life of poverty that we might receive the riches of his grace. As we considered that life, we learned to appreciate him and to call on Jesus as our saviour. As we face the future, we see that he has gone ahead of us. By God's decree he is the Lord of the future too, and he moves to meet and welcome us into the presence of his eternal day.

It is not surprising that what is probably one of the earliest Christian prayers is an urgent appeal – *maranatha*, 'Come, O Lord!' (1 Corinthians 16:22; cf. Revelation 22:20). This is an Aramaic word (or more correctly, two Aramaic words run together), and so is likely to go back to the first Jerusalem-based community. Scholars are not in full agreement as to how it should be translated, because it could also be translated as a statement – 'our Lord has come'. But the context in which it is used favours the prayer form. (For a summary of the points at issue see C. Brown, ed., *The New International Dictionary of New*

Testament Theology, Exeter, 1976, volume 2, pp. 895–898.)

It therefore looks as though from the very first the Christian church eagerly looked forward to the day when the Lord would merge the future with the present, finally removing all that still seeks to thwart his just rule and when at last 'we will be with the Lord for ever' (1 Thessalonians 4:17). It is a prayer which countless generations since have echoed, each in their own language, not least in times of oppression when we cry out for a future which will set right the evident injustices of the present.

'Jesus is Lord' – of the future too! As I have tried to emphasize, that is not an escape from the present. It is not an excuse to get round the responsibilities which we all share as members of a suffering and anxious humanity. It does mean, however, that we can face up to the challenge of the immediate future. We have a sure and certain hope that our ultimate destiny is secure in the hands of one whose authority is supreme. His purposes have been shown in history to be those of costly service in the interests of others. The Lordship of Jesus thus liberates us from yet another threat which might otherwise hold us in its grip. We are free to grow towards the full realization of our potential to be the responsible individuals that God created us to be.

8
GUIDELINES FOR CONSCIENCE

In matters of conscience we are not compelled to follow the crowd, even the holy crowd! It is a great relief to know that we can look to Jesus to set the compass of our consciences. We are not enslaved to peer pressure. Jesus' Lordship sets us free.

So far, we have been thinking about what it means to affirm that Jesus is Lord in the face of various threatening forces that come at us from outside. Now I want to turn to our relationships with other people. It may at first seem rather surprising that we should start with our relationships with our fellow Christians, but that is the setting for Paul's emphatic assertion of the Lordship of Jesus in Romans 14:9. We need, once again, to look at the wider context in which this verse is set to see why this should be so.

In Romans 14, Paul deals with the very real problems which can emerge when equally sincere members of the same congregation adopt different attitudes to certain issues. They need not be fundamental to our faith, but we believe them to be an important part of the living out of our Christian beliefs.

The two examples which he takes are ones which until

recently did not much concern the modern church, though there are signs that they may be coming to the fore again. I ought to make it clear, therefore, that I am using these two issues merely as examples of general principles and that I am not taking sides over the particular questions themselves.

VEGETABLES AND HOLY DAYS

The first example Paul uses concerns our diet: one Christian sees no difficulty about eating anything (within reason!), while another prefers to be a vegetarian (verse 2). Unlike our own day, this problem did not arise out of a concern for the animals themselves – as a protest against the practice of factory farming, for instance. One just did not know where the meat had come from or, in the case of those who came from a Jewish background, whether it had been properly slaughtered and prepared (see, for instance, 1 Corinthians 8 – 10). Meat bought on the open market might at some stage have been used as part of a pagan sacrifice. In such a case, it is understandable that some Christians preferred to have nothing to do with it. They did not want to give people the impression that they were in any way involved in such practices, or perhaps they even thought that the meat itself had somehow become contaminated by its involvement in these rites.

The other example Paul uses concerns the observance of days (verse 5). Some Christians regarded all days alike, while others had something like a religious calendar, treating certain days (whether one day a week or certain particular days in the year) as in some way special.

It may seem odd to us that these two examples were so fiercely controversial in the early church. Paul had his work cut out to prevent churches splitting up over them, but it is not difficult to think of more modern examples of the same sort of thing and, sadly, of congregations which have divided over such matters. But I do not think it would help us in what needs to be a calm discussion of the underlying principles at stake to list such examples. It might make you as hot under the collar as some of Paul's first readers evidently were! So let us stick for the moment to the important points he is trying to make here.

For simplicity's sake, Paul divides the church into two groups on the basis of the attitudes they adopt to these questions. (In practice, of course, things may have been rather more complicated than that – they often are!) On the one hand, he calls those who prefer not to eat meat 'weak' (verse 2). That does not mean that they were weak Christians, but rather that they had a 'weak', or as we might say, a tender conscience. Indeed, from another point of view, such people could be called (and would doubtless consider themselves to be) very strong Christians. They know what they believe, and often express those beliefs very forcefully. So we must not misunderstand Paul when he calls them 'weak'.

Interestingly, neither in this chapter nor in 1 Corinthians 8 – 10 does Paul call the other group 'strong', as we might expect. Whatever label he might have given them, clearly there was a group whom he distinguished from the weak, and for the sake of clarity and simplicity, I will refer to them as the 'strong'.

Now, it seems that in the church then as now, these two groups tended to adopt characteristic attitudes towards one another, and Paul condemns them both for this in verse 3. On the one hand, the strong tend to look down on the weak. Even if they do not say so out loud, their attitude is, 'Oh, you're not still hung up over that old-fashioned problem, are you? I thought we had grown out of that ages ago.'

The weak, on the other hand, have a tendency to 'condemn', that is, to criticize the strong. 'Do you know what I heard so-and-so does? What a disgrace! And then he has the nerve to come to church and call himself a Christian.' Perhaps you are a bit inconsistent like me and have caught yourself saying both things on different occasions, depending on what the particular issue is. Well, Paul will have none of it. Neither attitude is right, he argues, for it remains true in both cases that 'God has accepted him'.

THE POWER OF PEER PRESSURE

Fine, you say, but what on earth has all this got to do with the Lordship of Christ? 'Much in every way!', for

Paul now goes on to remind us how much these different attitudes within the church affect the way that we live. I am quite sure that there are large numbers of Christians who either do things they would prefer not to, or refrain from things which in themselves cause them no problem at all, for all the wrong reasons.

As we shall see in a minute, there are times when of course I must take care not to offend my fellow Christian. But that is very different from being browbeaten against our better judgment into a certain way of life, either because of some bully of a so-called Christian leader (and that is not too strong a term in some cases I have observed), or because of what is often called 'peer pressure', the overpowering fear of not conforming to the standards of a particular group. We should not minimize these pressures. Remember that often Christians look to their local church as the centre of their social as well as their more narrowly religious life. They may not have any close friends outside that circle, so that the pressure on them to conform to what they think is expected of them in all sorts of ways can be enormous. And it is the fears and insecurity that lurk behind the conformity of such believers that Paul is most anxious to do away with.

To do so, he effectively challenges us all to answer the question, whose servant are you? And whose servant do we think our fellow Christian is? Ours? Or the Lord's? Look at it from the human point of view, he urges. None of us would think of criticizing someone else's servant, because that servant is not answerable to you, but to his or her own master (verse 4). Let me give an example.

When I was a boy, growing up in North London, my mother was fortunate enough to have the help of a cleaner three mornings a week. Our Mrs Housden was a real treasure, fiercely loyal, hard-working, and devoted to the family. She had a pretty sharp tongue, as I well remember, but we wouldn't have been without her for anything. Now, Mrs Housden's pride and joy was our front doorstep. It was made of small red tiles, and always before she left Mrs Housden would polish that step until it was as shiny as a skating rink. The only trouble with it was that it was on a slope, so that it had to be negotiated with some care after it had received its thrice-weekly polishing! More than one of us had forgotten that in our haste and come to grief.

Now let us suppose that one day one of my somewhat frail elderly relatives was expected for tea. On such an occasion, my mother might quite well have asked Mrs Housden not to polish the step. Would one of our neighbours then have criticized her for not carrying out what they considered to be her duties? The response they would have received if they had made so bold does not bear repeating! 'To her own mistress she stood or fell' (and so did the elderly relative!).

FREED FROM WHAT OTHER PEOPLE THINK

There are not enough Mrs Housdens in our churches today, doing what they know to be right despite criticism. And there are too many 'neighbours' always ready to criticize others. 'For this very reason', and here we come to the heart of the matter, 'For this very reason, Christ died and returned to life so that *he* [and no-one else] might be the Lord of both the dead and the living' (verse 9). In other words, the Lordship of Christ ought to set us free from the fear of what anybody else thinks about us, provided, of course, that we are obedient and loyal to him. That is the drift of Paul's argument in verses 6–8. Whether the Christian (in terms of the examples Paul has been using) does or does not eat meat, whether he does or does not observe a particular day as part of his religious practice, what matters is that he should do it or not do it 'to the Lord', and be able honestly to give thanks to the Lord for the course of action adopted. 'Whether we live or die,' he concludes, 'we belong to the Lord', and it is a great deal less intimidating to serve him than to serve the fickle moods of our fellow Christians.

How might this work out in the practice of church life today? First, it should at once remove the criticism that so-and-so doesn't do much in the church. The basis for assessing what Christian service means (which this kind of criticism implies) is far too narrow. It suggests that the only way of telling whether someone is truly following the Lord is how many 'jobs' they do in the church. In reality we should be serving God with the whole of our lives – including our responsibilities to our families and homes, to our colleagues (and bosses) at work, and to the use of our leisure time. And what this means in any individual case may well be very different from any other.

None of us has the information available to pass judgment on what this may mean for another member of our congregation. These matters are intensely private. How often we say, 'Well, that's between you and the Lord', and then immediately go on to try to usurp the Lord's position in that relationship by making our own uninformed opinions on the matter all too clear.

9
'THE MRS HOUSDEN PRINCIPLE'

We have no right to push others about, to tell them how to behave or what jobs they should do. And we may need to risk the church's disapproval; to say 'No' to a preaching engagement and 'Yes' to playing with the children. What matters is love, not power.

Just yesterday, I was reading of a case that illustrates the 'Mrs Housden principle' very well. I quote it exactly as I read it.

In the South of England live a husband and wife, with her elderly father. When her father became ill, the woman decided she must give up her prominent leadership role in her local church in order to care for him, which deeply disappointed the congregation. When he became too much for her to handle and a nursing home seemed the only easy option, her husband took early retirement from his work instead, to join her in looking after the old man. Having been one step away from a major business appointment, his colleagues regarded this as madness. Because the task of nursing is now so arduous, they only manage to attend church one week in three, and never together. There is an unspoken attitude among the congregation that they are letting the church down, or maybe that their faith has lost its urgency. Because they have decided to give everything to this act of service they are no longer important people.

I am not suggesting that this would be the right course of action for every couple if faced with similar circumstances. On the basis of what Paul teaches, though, I do insist that if a couple felt that the Lord was calling them to an act of such self-sacrificial service they should receive the support, and not the criticism, of the local church.

It follows from this that we all, and church leaders in particular, should be very careful not to put heavy-handed pressure on any individual to do some particular 'job', however good in itself, in the church. We may suggest it, or point out the need and encourage someone to see that they may have the appropriate gifts to do something, but beyond that let our watchword be 'to his own master he stands or falls' (Romans 14:4).

Secondly, what I have just been emphasizing is not an excuse for laziness or not getting involved when and where we can. As Romans 14 continues, we find in verses 10–12 that Paul reminds us that 'we will all stand before God's judgment seat', and that 'each of us will give an account of himself to God.' The point here is twofold. On the one hand, as we have seen, because the Lord is to be our judge we have no right to usurp that position and to become someone else's judge. On the other hand, however, we must never forget that we ourselves are all responsible for the lives that we live as servants of that same Lord. And of course, life in this context is not restricted to what might narrowly be called our church lives. It includes everything that we do and are.

So we gladly receive the freedom from fear of others that the teaching of the Lordship of Christ brings. But we must also accept the other side of that coin and be prayerfully thoughtful to order our lives in conscious obedience to his will. The fact that (in an ideal church!) we should not be criticized for what we decide to do or not do does not mean that we can use this as an excuse for just opting out. Most of us, I suspect, have sometimes been guilty of pandering to our own comfort by refusing to undertake tasks which in our heart of hearts we know the Lord is calling us to.

TAKING EASY OPTIONS

On other occasions we may have been equally guilty of committing ourselves to tasks which seem to be good, but which in fact are easier than some other less glamorous option. When our family were much younger, for instance, I had always to be careful when accepting an invitation to preach that I was not using it as a 'holy' excuse for avoiding my full share in the job of caring for our children. I cannot say that I always got the balance right in this – and I am sure that my wife, who has always been supportive beyond the call of duty, would say amen to that! And so I gradually learned that part of my obedience to my Lord was to consult fully with her before filling up my diary. How much more should this be the case when offering to do something which may demand a commitment outside the home of one or two evenings a week, year in and year out.

As each of us works out what the immediate Lordship of Christ means, we have to consider our lives as a whole and to seek his direction in ordering our priorities. The consequences of that will differ widely from one person to another, so once again let us conclude with Paul's practical words from this chapter: 'Each one should be fully convinced in his own mind' (verse 5).

There is a third and final consequence of all this. It may be the most difficult lesson to learn, or at least to apply, because it complicates the balance that I have just been talking about. It is that the Lordship of Christ should also give us freedom from the urge constantly to push our own rights in our dealings with other people. That urge is often no more than a thin veil for our sense of insecurity, on a par with the famous (but I hope apocryphal) comment in the preacher's notes: 'argument weak here, so bang the side of the pulpit.'

Paul was free from that in a way that Professor F. F. Bruce has memorably expressed in his commentary on this chapter:

> Paul enjoyed his Christian liberty to the full. Never was there a Christian more thoroughly emancipated from un-Christian inhibitions and taboos. So completely emancipated was he from spiritual bondage that he was not even in bondage to his emancipation. (*The Epistle of Paul to the Romans*, London, 1963, p. 243)

Sadly, it is possible so to grasp the truth of the freedom from fear of others in the church that we ram it down their throats and make life a misery for the rest of the congregation. The difficulty becomes one of knowing where to draw the line between standing firm for the truth of the gospel and at the same time striving to 'live at peace with everyone' (Romans 12:18), of insisting that Jesus alone is our Lord while in the same breath looking 'not only to your own interests, but also to the interests of others' (Philippians 2:4).

FIRST OF ALL PRINCIPLES: LOVE

Here again is a delicate path which each of us has to tread in obedience to Christ. Part of any decision has to be the impact which it will make on my fellow Christian. That might at first seem to stand on its head what we were looking at earlier, but a moment's thought will make clear that this is not really so. The Lordship of Christ is not, as we have seen, an excuse for just having everything our own way. In fact, just the opposite – it should set us free from any lesser constraint so that we really are in a position to have it all *his* way. Only then do we have any right to ignore what could otherwise be hurtful criticism.

Clearly, the working out of that Lordship as it affects me personally is never going to overturn the general guidelines which Christ has so painstakingly laid out for us by the example of his own life and teaching. And the first is the overriding command to love. So I can be quite sure that if I do something which does not spring from and end up in love, then it is no part of my obedience to Christ.

As we are often correctly reminded, 'love' in this context is not always an easy option. It does not mean that we may never need to be controversial, or that we simply always go along with the majority and never rock the boat. We know that all too well from many everyday examples, such as the bringing up of children, where the loving thing to do may be painful for the child in the short run because of its long-term benefits. It is not loving to let someone else do whatever they want, even if it will clearly end up in their own hurt for a while.

So too in the church. If at the time of the Reformation Luther had kept quiet about the truths of the gospel that he had freshly perceived from his study of Scripture, because people might find them upsetting, we should never have been in a position to consider this question today at all! So love is not necessarily a soft option. But we need to examine our motives extremely carefully. When we take a stand on a matter of principle it must be genuinely because of concern for others' well-being and not just to push ourselves into the limelight. It is not for us to justify some personal ambition or selfish course of action, still less to cover up a sense of insecurity that we might be wrong after all.

In the second half of Romans 14, Paul explains this principle with reference to the examples that he had used earlier in the passage. Instead of judging one another, he says, we should 'judge' rather that we do not put some unnecessary cause of offence in our fellow Christian's path (verse 13). Paul is fully persuaded in his own mind that there is nothing wrong with eating meat; he does not consider himself one of the 'weak' in the sense that we discussed earlier (verse 14). 'But,' he says, 'if your brother is distressed because of what you eat, you are no longer acting in love' (verse 15), and the result of that can be that something which is actually good in itself turns out to be considered evil (verse 16).

So once again it boils down to a question of priorities. 'Righteousness, peace and joy in the Holy Spirit' should rank higher than personal considerations about what to eat and drink (verse 17). Do not let hang-ups about lesser things destroy God's greater work of building up one another's Christian character (verses 19–20). A delicate balance is called for here, and each one of us has to be fully assured in our own minds before God.

Rigorous honesty is necessary. It is all too easy to deceive ourselves. But awareness of the problem is part of the first step towards solving it. And in the meantime we can rejoice again in the fact that it is to the Lord Jesus Christ that we must answer for the conclusions that we reach and not to our less well-informed fellow Christians. In matters of conscience we are told to love them, but to render obedience to Christ alone. Truly, we can thank God for that!

10
LORD OF OUR PERSECUTORS

Christians have always struggled to do what their Lord wants – and have always suffered because state and society hate this witness. But we fear persecution. Who wouldn't? If we first fear the Lord, however, these other fears fall into place.

In the last chapter, we looked at the way in which we can all be influenced into acting against our better judgment because of anxiety over what other Christians may think about us. Now we turn to consider another and potentially far worse fear, namely what those outside the church may both say and do to us.

Before we begin, I ought to say that I am very conscious of not being at all well qualified to write about this subject. Throughout the history of the church, and still in many parts of the world today, innumerable Christians have suffered all manner of persecution. Some have been martyred, others tortured and imprisoned, and still others have been psychologically severely assaulted on account of their Christian faith. This was true already in the days of the New Testament. I have not been through anything even remotely resembling that, though I have been humbled when meeting a few who have.

In the comparatively comfortable Britain of the late twentieth century, I have listened to sermons on biblical passages which deal with these subjects. They often 'interpret' them in terms of the unpopularity which may sometimes be our lot or of the sense of pain which we may experience when even quite close friends or members of our family reject our presentation of the Christian gospel. But how tame, even hollow, such an application must seem to anyone whose faith has been tested in the furnace of real persecution. Of course, preachers have a duty to apply the message of the Bible in ways that are relevant to the circumstances of those who listen to them, but we must not pretend, even to ourselves, that this is the same thing.

We certainly have no right to pontificate from our privileged but inexperienced position about what precise course of action others should take. Nor should we criticize those who in times of trial have reacted in ways that we do not fully understand. The situations that many have to face are too terrifying for any one of us to know how we would react in the same situation. We marvel at the courage that many have shown and are inspired by their example.

In tackling this subject, then, we can certainly see what the New Testament has to say about it. I hope that we may be able to draw out some general principles which are applicable to us no matter what our personal situation may be. But beyond that, let us pray that we never have to face the problem with the severity that others have known. If we do, may we be given grace to know what we ought to do and the necessary courage to see it through.

Of one thing we can be sure, however. If the Bible teaches a certain course of action for those who really were facing persecution, how much more should we be challenged by that teaching when the consequences of following it are likely to be so much easier for us.

PETER ON PERSECUTION

The first letter of Peter was written from Rome (that is the significance of 'Babylon' in 5:13) to persecuted Christians in various parts of what we call Turkey (1:1). It is not clear, however, whether this was a systematic and official persecution such as beset the church on at least one occasion in the first century. It might have been more a case of unofficial and sporadic local opposition which overwhelmed many of the new young churches.

The readers are offered various forms of encouragement as they face this ordeal. They are reminded, for instance, of their eternal inheritance which nothing in this present life can take away (chapter 1), and of the fact that, so far as possible, Christians should avoid unnecessary persecution by being obedient to their human overlords (2:13ff.). Above all, they are reminded several times of the example of Jesus himself who suffered unjustly at the hands of men, thus leaving them an example to follow in their loyalty to him (e.g. 2:21–25; 3:18).

In 3:13–17, however, a more specific situation seems to be in view, and so appropriately more specific instructions are given. It appears that some Christians may find themselves being put on trial in a court of law on some charge arising out of their practice of the faith. That, at any rate, is the easiest way of understanding the meaning of 'to give an answer' (i.e. to defend yourself) in verse 15, and of 'those who speak maliciously against' (i.e. accuse) in verse 16. Of course, this might be more of a 'kangaroo court' than a properly constituted one, but the underlying point will remain the same.

Here, it is repeatedly assumed that they are not facing charges of actual wrongdoing. This passage certainly cannot be applied to those who have simply fallen foul of the legitimate laws of the land! It applies only if 'you should suffer for what is right' (verse 14), 'if you are eager to do good' (verse 13), and if 'keeping a clear conscience . . . [you] suffer for doing good [rather] than for doing evil' (verses 16–17). The point could hardly be more emphatically made.

Sometimes, however, the accusation may be brought for no legitimate reason, but purely because of the accused's practice of the Christian faith. In these circumstances, the Christian should certainly speak in his or her own defence, explaining clearly what the truth of the matter is, but doing so 'with gentleness and respect' (verse 15). Moreover, the blameless public life of a Christian ought to be sufficient to show up the false nature of the accusation that is levelled against them (verse 16).

Sometimes, however, human prejudice and bigotry are such that not even this may be sufficient to save the accused from suffering (verse 17). To such people, there is the promise of a very special blessing, which our Lord himself first pronounced (Matthew 5:10–12) and which is echoed both in verse 14 of our passage and in other parts of the New Testament such as James 5:11; Revelation 2:10; 6:9–11; and 7:14–17.

Jesus himself knew that his followers would sometimes be subjected to this form of trial. When he spoke about the need to proclaim the gospel to all nations and that a consequence of this might be that 'brother will betray brother to death', he told them, 'Whenever you are arrested and brought to trial, do not worry beforehand about what to say. Just say whatever is given you at the time, for it is not you speaking, but the Holy Spirit' (Mark 13:11). And in the book of Acts, we have the examples of Peter and John (chapters 4 and 5), of Stephen (chapter 7), and of Paul (chapters 22–24 and 26) facing just such situations.

PREPARING FOR TRIALS

If, then, a Christian on trial is not to 'worry beforehand' but to look to the Holy Spirit for the words to say, how should preparation for the trial be made? It does not mean that one should not prepare carefully if time permits – Paul certainly had more than adequate time to think through what he was going to say during the more than two years of his imprisonment at Caesarea (Acts 24:27)! But that is hardly the main point. In any case, Peter's readers are urged, 'Always be prepared to give an answer to everyone who asks you to give the reason for the hope that you have' (3:15). Before that, however, they are told what really matters, namely to 'in your hearts set apart Christ as Lord', and in contrast, 'Do not fear what they fear; do not be frightened'.

Now, on the face of it that seems like pretty impractical advice. After all, these people are on trial, possibly for their lives, so how can such pious sentiments be of any help whatsoever? Well, look at Peter's words in the light of all that we have been studying in this book. On each occasion where we have looked at the context of the claim that Jesus (or in this case Christ) is Lord, we have found a rival power that seeks to dominate our lives through force or fear. Clearly, the same is true of this passage also.

More than that, however, it is quite possible that we are dealing here with an even more specific threat than just the fact of being falsely accused. We know that on a number of occasions Christians were 'caught out' by being forced to express their loyalty to the Roman empire by affirming that Caesar (i.e. the emperor, whatever his actual name was) is god. This was the official religious position. In fact there were some religions, of which Judaism was a notable example, which were exempt from making this affirmation which so clearly ran counter to their deepest convictions. The position of Christianity in its early days was not clear in this regard. This was exploited by some local officials, for clearly no Christian, any more than any Jew, could recognize Caesar as God.

Perhaps, then, the Christians to whom Peter was writing were facing the prospect of having to make this blasphemous assertion in court, in which case they are urged to sanctify in their hearts Christ – and not Caesar – as Lord. If so, as with the other passages we have looked at, the emphasis in reading should be on the word 'Christ' rather than on the word 'Lord'. Only with such a clear sense of where their loyalties lay could they rely with confidence on the gift of the Spirit to guide them as they spoke in their defence – but what confidence such a 'defence lawyer' would inspire!

Linked with this, secondly, is the astonishing assurance that they need 'not fear what they fear; do not be frightened'. This is actually a quotation from Isaiah 8:12, and the next verse there goes on in rather the same vein as the passage in 1 Peter, except that in Isaiah, of course, the prophet speaks of regarding God as holy whereas the New Testament writer refers to Christ as holy – a clear pointer to the divinity of Jesus Christ in his view. However, Isaiah continues with words that help to explain our passage in 1 Peter a bit further: 'The LORD Almighty is the one you are to regard as holy, he is the one you are to fear, he is the one you are to dread.' In other words, as G. T. Smart once wrote in his well-known hymn, 'Through all the changing scenes of life', it is a case of

'Fear him, ye saints, and you will then
have nothing else to fear.'

11

DANIEL'S DREAM

The picture-language of Daniel's dream describes two quite opposite invisible worlds. In one the brute beasts rule in power; in the other the glorious figure of the Son of Man exercises a love-based authority. Which Lordship is more attractive?

How would thoughts of God have helped the early Christians to face such trials without fear, and can we too recapture something of their outlook in our very different circumstances? To answer this question, we need to understand that the idea of the people of God facing tremendous pressure and threat from ungodly civil powers was nothing new. It was a problem that the Jews too had to face towards the end of the Old Testament period. There is plenty of evidence to show that the early church responded in some respects by drawing on the same theological resources.

Let me take one prominent example in order to show what I mean – the strange chapter 7 of the book of Daniel. Of course, many Bible students have had a field day with this chapter, using it to try to predict all sorts of goings on in the world (I won't embarrass anyone by naming them or describing their particular ideas!). This, however, is to miss the whole point of what the writer is trying to get across.

In this chapter, Daniel has a dream. He sees the 'great sea' which is being whipped up by strong winds from all four points of the compass (verse 2). The scene, therefore, is one of frightening chaos and of uncontrollable forces. Remember that the ancient Israelites were not a sea-faring people, and indeed regarded the sea with a considerable degree of dread and suspicion. The original readers of this passage would have at once seen in this picture a symbol of the restless and rebellious nations of the world who generally go about their business without regard for God. The writer of Psalm 2 uses a similar idea:

> Why do the nations conspire
> and the peoples plot in vain?
> The kings of the earth take their stand
> and the rulers gather together against the
> LORD,
> and against his Anointed One.

Out of this chaotic sea, then, Daniel sees four 'beasts' rising up one after the other, and later on, in verse 17, we are told that these represent four different kingdoms. Although it is true that they are said to be different from one another (verse 3), we should not overlook the fact that they share certain features in common. In particular, each wields oppressive power, which it exercises in its own individual way, 'eating its fill', 'crushing in pieces', 'trampling underfoot', or whatever. There are several things we need to notice about these beasts.

BRUTES IN CHARGE

First, they contradict God's original intention in creating the world. In Genesis 1, we are told that mankind, made in the image and likeness of God, was given authority over the animal kingdom. This was not, of course, in order to exploit it, but as God's representatives on earth to care for it and administer it on his behalf. So when brute beasts exercise dominion over humanity, that is an exact reversal of how things ought to be. And in the picture-world of Daniel's dream, it is not difficult to apply the lesson to the affairs of nations. In the international scene of both ancient and modern times, naked power is often much admired almost for its own sake. This leads to the denial of genuinely human values, such as individuality, compassion for the underprivileged, the expression of creativity in artistic and other ways, the freedom to think without fear or favour. These and other values stand in the way of much aggressive political ambition and so have to be crushed as though they were nothing more than a minor inconvenience. The monstrous bestiality of Daniel's dream is as telling a symbol today as it was then.

Second, there seems to be a deterioration through the description of the four beasts. The first one, the lion, is made to stand upon two feet like a man, and a man's heart (i.e. mind) was given to it. So it has some semblance of humanity. From the fourth beast, however, there comes a little horn, and 'this horn had eyes like the eyes of a man and a mouth that spoke boastfully' (verse 8). What a grotesque picture! Apparently human characteristics, yes, but now perverted and misused to the point of revulsion.

Surely this too is true to experience. It has always seemed to those who suffer under such regimes that the present is far worse than anything that has gone before. And that, I suggest, is not mere ancient history. Mankind has increasingly learned how to use his dominion over nature to devise ever more sophisticated methods of manipulation and oppression.

THE SON OF MAN

At this point, the scene of Daniel's dream shifts to the courts of heaven, where in verse 13 we are introduced to a different figure, 'one like a son of man'. Let us try to empty our minds of the use of that phrase by Jesus and try to understand it in the context which we have already been considering. In every way this figure contrasts with the beasts. His character is different – 'a son of man' means, in the idiom of the language of the Old Testament, one who partakes of the character of a man; in other words, he is genuinely human in the sense that God intended humanity to be. His origin is different – he comes 'with the clouds of heaven', and not from the chaotic sea which gave rise to the beasts. And his authority is different – not temporary, as the authority of the beasts is said to be (verses 11–12), but eternal. 'His dominion is an everlasting dominion that will not pass away, and his kingdom is one that will never be destroyed' (verse 14). So true humanity is to be sharply distinguished from all that has gone before.

Now, here is something very curious, for when the interpretation of this scene is given later in the chapter, there is no direct reference to this figure. Instead, in his place we find 'the saints of the Most High' (verse 22). They are the faithful people of God, and their identity with him is shown by the fact that it is *their* dominion and kingdom which is going to be everlasting. And the puzzle does not quite end there, for the interpretation tells us more about these 'saints' than the original vision had led us to expect. Verses 21 and 25 show us that they are the very ones who are caught up in the contemporary history as the oppressed people of God.

This difference between the vision and its interpretation is not accidental. In the world of the beasts, the saints are simply overlooked, but in the world of heaven they constitute the very centre of attention.

So what have we learned from this digression into Daniel 7? Hopefully, its picture-language has impressed forcibly upon us that there are two worlds, and that they are completely incompatible. As so often, this comes most sharply into focus in the life and ministry of Jesus. As is well known, he used the title 'son of man' as a way of referring to himself, but closer study shows that he used it in two ways.

Sometimes, he used it in connection with his suffering, and on other occasions he used it to refer to his future triumph. In this, I believe it is legitimate to see him as (amongst many other things) a representative figure, rather like the 'one like a son of man' is in Daniel's vision. Like many of his later followers, he too first went the way of suffering and oppression. His significance was written off and denied both by the Romans and by many others of his contemporaries, and this led inexorably, as we know, to the cross. The 'little horn' seemed at first to prevail. But there are two worlds! And for those with eyes to see, Jesus displayed all the qualities of that true humanity which God always intended. He drew his authority not from earthly motivated might and power, but from submission and obedience to the will of God. Consequently, in his resurrection and ascension, he was vindicated in the world that really matters, the world of God and of eternity. That vindication, he taught by the use of the second group of 'son of man' sayings, will one day be openly displayed for all to see.

Returning now to the letter of 1 Peter, I have no doubt that its first readers would have been familiar with the kind of thought-world which we have been discussing. Faced with the mighty 'beast' of imperial Rome, they are encouraged to look away to the world of the son of man: 'in your hearts set apart *Christ* as Lord' (1 Peter 3:15). In your trial, there are values at stake which transcend the immediate present. Christ's obedient pathway to the cross has ensured that the humanity of the people of God will prevail.

But this is *not*, I must insist, a trite other-worldly escapism. It was in this world that Christ suffered, leaving us an example that we should walk in his steps (1 Peter 2:21). The two worlds are but two ways of looking at the same reality. It is not a case of 'here and then there', 'now and then in the time to come'. And it is because this is so that the teaching of this passage actually reaches beyond the immediate confines of Christians on trial in the first or any other century. It speaks to us all, whatever circumstances we currently find ourselves in.

Inhuman beasts of aggression and oppression are everywhere and at all times opposed to the godly humanity of the saints, and to that extent we are all on trial every moment of our lives. Caesar and the son of man – they stand for worlds which constantly confront us with a choice about values. The forces that would pressurize us into conformity with the sub-human beasts may not be so physically terrifying as those of Daniel 7 or 1 Peter 3, but they are every bit as powerful and menacing, for all their more subtle and humane (but not human!) disguise. So 'in your hearts set apart Christ as Lord'.

12

CONFIDENT WITNESSES

In the face of an unbelieving and jeering world, telling the good news of Jesus can be painfully hard. But Jesus has overcome that very world. All he asks is that we speak about what he has done, not to invent theology; and he will be there with us.

There is one further theme that we need to examine, and that is the issue of authority. So far, we have been thinking in terms of how fear of other people comes at us head on. Confrontation has been the name of the game. We have seen that for the Christian all is not necessarily as it might at first seem on the surface of things. Now, it will be worthwhile to see how a grasp of the Lordship of Christ can also encourage us as we move from the defensive role of prisoner in the dock into the more positive role of witnesses and ambassadors for Christ. In the work of evangelism, too, our fear of what others may say or think can also be strongly inhibiting. Is there anything in what we have been considering that can help us with this familiar problem?

JESUS AND THE TWO WORLDS

We must look a bit further at how the authority of Jesus relates to the business of the two worlds that we were discussing earlier. It is a prominent theme in

Matthew's gospel. At the start of his earthly ministry, as is well known, we have the account of how Jesus was tempted by Satan. It is interesting to notice that Matthew puts the three temptations in a different order from Luke. In Luke 4:1–13, we find first the temptation to make stones into bread, then the one where Jesus is shown all the kingdoms of the world and promised authority over them, and finally the temptation to throw himself down from the highest point of the temple. In Matthew 4:1–11, however, these last two come in reverse order. It looks as though Matthew wants us to regard the one about the kingdoms of the world as the climax of the series.

Looking at it in more detail, we find that in this temptation Jesus is taken up to 'a very high mountain' and shown 'all the kingdoms of the world and their splendour' (verse 8). He is promised that if he will only bow down and worship Satan, they will all be given to him. From this we learn, then, that Satan has a considerable measure of authority in the realm of these kingdoms. What is more, we might at first think that for Jesus to get in on this act would be very attractive to him (it wouldn't have been much of a temptation otherwise). After all, did he not come to earth for just this reason?

But what sort of authority is being talked about here? Is it not exactly the same kind that was exercised by the beasts of Daniel 7? Of course there is a way to gain authority of a sort by brute force, but it maintains its power through the rule of fear and terror. And that is the very opposite of the nature of the rule of God in his kingdom.

Immediately before this passage, we have the story of Jesus' baptism when he heard the voice from the father declaring, 'This is my Son, whom I love; with him I am well pleased' (3:17). Will the son walk the way of the father? This was the nature of the test that Jesus confronted on that lonely mountain. It was not so much about whether he would gain authority, but what sort of authority it would be – the one achieved by the easy path of terrorism, or the authority of love that could be won only by the hard path which led to the cross.

Jesus' answer was emphatic, though he knew how costly it would be: 'Away from me, Satan! For it is written: "Worship the Lord your God, and serve him only"' (verse 10). That decision was to have consequences which go beyond just 'the kingdoms of the world'.

But first, let us just notice briefly how in the following chapters of the gospel this theme of authority is developed, especially as it relates to the disciples as they are taught the way of mission. First, Jesus *declares* his authority over them so that he can use them in the spread of the kingdom: 'Come, follow me, and I will make you fishers of men' (4:19), a call which they willingly and spontaneously obey. Second, he *demonstrates* his authority to them in a number of ways – in teaching (7:29, with reference to the Sermon on the Mount in chapters 5–7), in healing (8:5–13; note this story is related to the issue of authority in verse 9), and in forgiveness (9:6). And then third, he *delegates* his authority to them as he sends them out in mission (10:1).

In all this, we can see how Jesus was teaching and demonstrating the nature of the authority which is operative in the kingdom of God. How different it is from that on which he had so resolutely turned his back in the course of the temptations! As yet, however, it was restricted to only a few, and was being exercised within a very small geographical and social area. In particular, he specifically tells his disciples that at this stage they should not 'go among the Gentiles or enter any town of the Samaritans. Go rather to the lost sheep of Israel' (10:5–6).

'GO AND MAKE DISCIPLES'

Compare all this now with the scene at the very end of the gospel after the Father's vindication of his path of obedience to the cross in the resurrection. Once again – as in that third temptation – we are taken up a mountain (28:16), but this time the disciples worship him (verse 17). 'Worship the Lord your God, and serve him only,' Jesus had replied to Satan on that earlier occasion. Now we find that he accepts their worship of him without let or hindrance.

What is more, he catches up the earlier theme of

authority with his words, 'All authority has been given to me'. On earth, as Satan had offered him? Yes, but not just that! 'All authority *in heaven* and on earth has been given to me' (verse 18). Here is something which Satan could never have given him, but because he had chosen to worship God alone to the point of obedience in death upon the cross, he is given authority in both 'worlds', in heaven as well as on earth.

Far-reaching consequences flow from that, as we can see from Jesus' next words. 'Therefore go and make disciples of all nations' (verse 19). In the first place, and perhaps easiest to grasp, is the extension of the disciples' mission from 'the lost sheep of Israel' to all the nations of the world. His victory is universal, and so appropriately it is to be proclaimed on a universal scale.

Even more striking, however, is the wealth of meaning contained in that little word 'therefore'. It is because of the scope and nature of the authority that Jesus has secured that the disciples can go out in the first place. This should directly affect our attitude to evangelism today. That is the theme of this chapter as a whole, namely what the Lordship of Christ means for our attitude towards those who are as yet outside of the church. First, it means that we have the right to go. Often, perhaps, we feel apologetic in our attitude towards evangelism, even embarrassed, as though we were intruding where we have no right to be. But

Jesus has 'all authority on earth', so that the answer to such feelings is to 'set him apart in our hearts as Lord' rather than our neighbour.

Secondly, Jesus' statement also gives us confidence as we go. This follows from the fact that he has 'authority in heaven'. The church is recapturing in our day that there is a spiritual warfare involved in the battle for people's hearts and affections. Only the one with authority in heaven is in a position to triumph in that warfare, and in fact he has already done so.

Sometimes Christians give the impression by the form of their prayers that a good deal hangs either on their own earnestness, or on their secret knowledge of some formula or spiritual technique that will persuade Jesus to come out of his shell to exercise his authority on their behalf in their evangelistic enterprises! But all such thinking is upside down. The authority is already his, and he sends us, we don't have to persuade him. To suggest anything less, however well intentioned, not only demonstrates a state of spiritual insecurity but borders on a dishonouring 'takeover bid' for Jesus' own power and authority.

Thirdly, we learn that evangelism is a proclamation of what Jesus has accomplished. It is not an attempt to make up on his behalf for something that is somehow lacking in the work that he has done. We cannot improve on his work by our efforts, and so we should not give that impression. We explain to people what their real needs are and we present to them the great solution that God has for them in Christ. For their own good, we may certainly persuade them of the need for response, but not give the idea that they will be doing God a favour by turning to him. 'All authority has been given to me . . . *Therefore* go . . . ' – there's a good deal of meaning packed into that single word, and it repays careful pondering.

Finally, remember the encouragement that he gives us as we face the outside world. In this chapter, we have seen something of the fears that can beset Christians in the face of encounter with non-Christians, with whom we are often hesitant to discuss our faith. We have also seen, however, that part of our problem is that our vision is too restricted. We think only in terms of a single world, whereas the imagery of a book like Daniel, to say nothing of the explicit language of the New Testament, makes clear that there is a fuller reality beyond the spheres of sense and sight. Since in this realm Jesus reigns supreme as authoritative Lord, it is vital that we have a right attitude towards him if we are to gain a right perspective on our 'external relations' in this present world as well.

If we do, however, then his promise follows: 'And surely I am with you always, to the very end of the age' (28:20). That was how the gospel started. In the Christmas story, it was said, 'They will call him Immanuel, which means, "God with us" ' (1:23). Jesus' first coming into this world spoke of the fact that God had not abandoned humanity but in Christ had come alongside his creation to 'save his people from their sins' (1:21). Now at the end, however, he does not desert us either! With his authority established, both in heaven and on earth, there is nowhere we can go, no situation in which we may find ourselves, no confrontation too severe or oppressive but our Lord is there. He is with us, for us, and wielding his authority on our behalf where the real action is and where it most matters – in the very courts of heaven itself.

13

GOD'S POWER FOR THE CHURCH

The New Testament calls Jesus 'head' rather than 'Lord' of the church, but it comes to the same thing. He gives us, as it were, the wind of his authority. We set our sails to catch that wind and go where he wants us to. 'Set your minds on things above.'

We have looked at what it means for our individual relationships, both within and outside the church, when we affirm that Jesus is Lord. Now we need to go a step further and discuss what it means for the church as a whole.

There is no statement in the New Testament (so far as I can see) which uses the phrase 'Jesus is Lord' in precisely this context. However, as we shall see, there is a passage which comes very close to it. Nor should we be surprised that things are a bit different in this sphere. We are not now dealing with individual believers, where the idea of Lordship is most appropriate. The church looks to the ascended and exalted Christ as its head; the emphasis is less on the earthly life of Jesus. The New Testament tends therefore to speak of Christ as the head of the church rather than of Jesus as its Lord.

The relevant passage comes at the end of Ephesians

chapter 1. The chapter as a whole divides into two main parts. In verses 3–14, Paul praises God for his work in the lives of all believers. This part of the chapter is rather like a hymn with three verses, each ending with a refrain 'to the praise of his glory' (verses 6, 12 and 14). The first 'verse' deals with the work of God the Father (verses 3–6), the second with the work of God the Son (verses 7–12), and the third with the work of God the Holy Spirit (verses 13–14). Because the whole passage is couched in the language of praise ('Praise be to the God and Father of our Lord Jesus Christ, who has . . .', verse 3), everything which is said here is true of all Christian believers. The triune God is being praised for what he has already done for each one of us.

In the second part of the chapter, however (verses 15–23), Paul goes on to pray for his readers. Having said that he thanks God for them, he then tells them that he mentions them in his prayers asking *that* . . . (verses 15–17). When we pray in this way, of course, we mean that we want something to change in the situation of the one for whom we are praying. If I pray *that* my wife may be healed of her migraines, I mean that I want them to stop!

There are two main things that Paul prays for in the lives of his readers – first that they may have 'a spirit of wisdom and revelation' in their knowledge of God (verse 17), and secondly that they may know three things. They probably knew something about them already, but Paul clearly thinks that it is important that they should understand them much better.

POWER AVAILABLE

The three things Paul wants them to know are (i) 'the hope to which he has called you'; (ii) 'the riches of his glorious inheritance in the saints' (both in verse 18); and (iii) 'his incomparably great power for us who believe' (verse 19). Now, each of these three points is quite involved and complicated, and we cannot hope to deal with them all here. Paul regarded the third point as the most important because he goes on to develop it through to the end of the chapter. So let us look more closely at this part of Paul's prayer.

As we have seen, Paul wants the Ephesians to know more of the great power of God which is available to believers. To explain what that power is, he refers to the way it has been demonstrated in the life and work of Christ. It has done three things, he reminds them: it has raised Christ from death (verse 20); it has seated him at God's right hand (verse 20); and it has subjected all things to him (verse 22). We need to unpack these statements a little if we too are to know more of the nature of the power of God.

The first point is the most obvious and the easiest one for us to grasp. If we were to be asked for an example of the demonstration of God's power at work in history we would probably think first of the resurrection of Jesus Christ from the dead. We thought about it earlier in terms of Christ's victory over 'King Death'. However, if we go on to ask exactly what power was at work on that first Easter morning, we may find ourselves a bit stuck for words. It is hardly something that can be quantified by some physical formula!

Things like this which go beyond our full comprehension are usually better expressed in poetry than coldly scientific statements. Some of the most evocative attempts to get to grips with it come in many of our Easter hymns. I am always rather sorry that whereas we seem to sing Christmas carols for weeks before (and sometimes after) Christmas Day, we tend to restrict Easter hymns to the day itself. As a result they are far less well-known than they ought to be, considering how central this truth is to our faith. One that has been an especial favourite of mine ever since boyhood captures in picture-language some-thing of the power of God at work in Christ's resurrection. It does so without actually mentioning either of those words themselves − such is the effectiveness of poetry that no further comment is needed!

> For Judah's Lion burst his chains
> And crushed the serpent's head;
> And cries aloud through death's domain
> To wake the imprisoned dead.

The second demonstration of the power of God is

that he has seated Christ 'at his right hand in the heavenly realms' (verse 20). The New Testament never stops with Christ only (!) raised from death but always presses on to speak in the same breath of his ascension, his return to the glory of heaven. They are two stages on the same journey, so to speak – from the depths of the grave to the heights of exaltation. We tend to think of them as separate, but from God's point of view they are one; the Jesus who was rejected on earth is accepted and given the place of greatest honour in heaven.

JESUS' WORK FOR US

Our first reaction to that idea might be one of disappointment. It seems to suggest that the Jesus whom we know as a man, the Jesus with whom it is easiest for us to identify, has been removed to a position far away. If he is 'seated at God's right hand' in heaven, then there is no way in which he can be close to us here on earth. In fact, however, it stresses that he has done, and is continuing to do, things that we need very much. Paradoxically enough, they bring him close to each one of us. Once again, we have to learn not to be put off by the picture-language, but rather to ask what the picture-language is trying to tell us.

COMPLETION

The letter to the Hebrews makes it clear first that it is a picture which speaks of *completion* – of a job well done. Verse 3 of the first chapter says, 'After he had provided purification for sins, he sat down at the right hand of the Majesty in heaven', and this is developed in verses 11–12 of chapter 10: 'Day after day every priest stands and performs his religious duties; again and again he offers the same sacrifices, which can never take away sins. But when this priest had offered for all time one sacrifice for sins, he sat down at the right hand of God.'

Standing and sitting make a good contrast in this passage. The priests of the Old Testament are pictured as standing because their work is never done; the sacrifices which they offer have to be repeated 'day after day', and even then they are not effective. But 'this priest', meaning Jesus, offered himself as a sacrifice in a way that never has to be repeated, emphasized by the fact of his sitting down.

This way of looking at the picture, then, brings peace to our troubled consciences. Nothing remains for us or anybody else to do in the fundamental problem of how to get rid of the sin which separates us from God.

COMFORT

From God's right hand Jesus is able to bring us *comfort*. This also gets mentioned in two places. In Romans 8:34 Paul tells us that the Jesus who died, rose and is at the right hand of God 'is also interceding for us', while in Hebrews again the writer, having pointed out our need for a high priest who will also intercede for us (7:23–28), goes on to affirm that 'The point of what we are saying is this: We do have such a high priest, who sat down at the right hand of the throne of the Majesty in heaven' (8:1).

In other words, the picture is now showing us a Jesus who is praying for us – and what better place could there be to pray effectively from than the right hand of God himself? I wonder what you think he is praying for in your case. I believe that the main point of his prayer is just the same as it was for Peter on the night Jesus was arrested and taken away for trial. You will remember what a traumatic night that was for Peter and the bitterness it brought him. He suddenly realized that Jesus had been only too accurate in his prediction that he, Peter, would deny his Lord three times. But even before that prediction was made, Jesus had said something else to Peter. 'Satan has asked to sift you as wheat. But I have prayed for you, Simon, that your faith may not fail' (Luke 22:31–32).

Yes, there are times – too many times, perhaps – when as Christians we too let our Lord down in ways that afterwards we deeply regret. But that does not mean that we are therefore beyond the pale, or that he will cut us off short. On the contrary! Even before it happens he has prayed that our faith will not fail. Faith, which we thought was up to us, is the very quality which is maintained by his faithfulness in prayer for us.

Cooperation

A third use of our picture phrase brings Jesus even closer to us. It talks of his *cooperation* with us as we go out to witness in his name. It comes at the end of Mark's gospel, and there are problems about whether this passage was an original part of the gospel or not. I do not intend to discuss that here because the truth of the point being made does not depend upon it.

In Mark 16:19 we find a reference to the ascension in just the terms which we are considering: 'He was taken up into heaven and he sat at the right hand of God'. But what a surprise the very next verse unfolds: 'Then the disciples went out and preached everywhere, and the Lord worked with them.'

It could not be stated more plainly that Jesus being at the right hand of God has not removed him from our experience. Rather, it must again be picture-language. He is now in a place of supreme authority from which he is the better able to empower us in his service, no matter where that may take us.

Consecration

There is one more passage to look at briefly before we return to our phrase in Ephesians 1. It is important that we should not overlook this one. It gives to the whole theme the balance which we so often find in the New Testament between teaching which brings us encouragement and a corresponding challenge to our present way of life. It comes at the beginning of

Colossians chapter 3. I want to suggest that Christ being at the right hand of God calls for *consecration* on our part. Let me quote the passage in full:

> Since, then, you have been raised with Christ, set your hearts on things above, where Christ is seated at the right hand of God. Set your minds on things above, not on earthly things. For you died, and your life is now hidden with Christ in God. When Christ, who is your life, appears, then you also will appear with him in glory. (Colossians 3:1–4)

There are several things to note about this rather difficult passage. First, it reminds us that as Christians we are 'in Christ', and that means that whatever has happened to him has also in some way happened to us. For an illustration, take this book that you are now reading. Suppose you are using a bookmark. When you have finished reading for the time being, you put the bookmark in place and then you close the book. The bookmark is now 'in book'. Wherever the book goes, the bookmark goes with it. If the book accidentally falls into the fire and is burnt, the bookmark is burnt as well. If you put the book into your briefcase or handbag, the bookmark goes there as well: it is 'in book'.

Somewhat similarly, you are 'in Christ', and so from God's point of view the death that he died for sin, for instance, is your death to sin as well. When he was raised to God's right hand in heaven, you were raised there as well. Paul says exactly that in Ephesians 2, right after the passage that we are mainly thinking about in this chapter. 'God raised us up with Christ and seated us with him in the heavenly realms *in* Christ Jesus' (Ephesians 2:6). That, then, is where we belong. To all outward appearances you may look just like anyone else, but 'you died, and your life is now hidden with Christ in God' (Colossians 3:3).

Second, however, we may feel that we do not live life on that level. We are so unworthy of what looks like the most terrific honour that we wonder whether it can really be true at all. But what is now hidden about us, sometimes hidden even from ourselves, will one day be seen openly. Notice that verse 4 does not say that we shall be changed on that day, rather that 'when Christ, who is your life, appears, then you also will appear with him in glory'. So not only do we belong at God's right hand, but we also already have a character, even if it is hidden, that suits that status. As John says in his first letter,

How great is the love the Father has lavished on us, that we should be called children of God! And that is what we are! . . . now we are children of God, and what we will be has not yet been made known. But we know that when he appears, we shall be like him, for we shall see him as he is. (1 John 3:1–2)

105

So both the past and the future are well taken care of; what, then, of the present? That is where the challenge to consecration that I mentioned earlier comes in. *Since* we have been raised with Christ, we must 'set our hearts on things above, where Christ is seated at the right hand of God' (Colossians 3:1). The wonder of what has been done to us in the past and the glorious prospect of what lies in the future should spur us to a new life now. Our position is in Christ, seated at God's right hand, so to use an old familiar saying, we must become what we already are.

'SET YOUR MINDS'

To develop this more fully, Paul goes on to say, 'Set your minds on things above' (verse 2). The use of the English translation 'set' suggests a helpful illustration. We sometimes use the word in the context of sailing; we talk about 'setting the sails'. The principle, of course, is simple. The wind at any given time blows from more or less the same direction, but you can sail a boat in almost any direction (even without the use of a rudder) by the different setting of the sails. If the sails are let out loose, the boat will run away downwind, but if they are hauled in close, the boat will sail more into the direction that the wind is coming from (though never straight into the wind, of course!).

Now, I like to think of the wind as a picture of the love of God which 'blows' true and constant from his heavenly throne. If we picture ourselves as boats, it blows upon us all equally. The question is, how are we 'setting the sails' of our minds and thoughts? Some people seem to turn their backs on God and, as it were, spread their sails wide and so are blown further and further away from the source of the wind. But this does not have to be. Those who have been gripped by the vision of what God has done for them in Christ can 'set their minds' accordingly, and sail, so to speak, closer and closer towards the direction from which the wind is coming.

It is as unlikely to be a totally straight course as it is that a boat could sail straight into the wind. But by tacking to and fro amidst the trials and encouragements of life, we nevertheless find that we are gradually getting closer. So while God's love remains constant, we too have a responsibility if we are to grow into the characters that God has prepared for us as his children, seated at his right hand. 'Set your minds on things above.'

14

GOD'S GIFT AND OUR RESPONSE

The resurrection removed Jesus from the grave so that God could give him to us, his church. Our response is not to be aggressive but to follow his way, the way of the cross. This 'way', the Christian way, needs to be clearly understood but also vibrantly lived.

You are probably thinking by now that we have strayed a long way from Paul's prayer in Ephesians chapter 1. So as we return to it, let me recap. Paul, you will remember, was praying that his readers would know more about various things, most especially the power of God. To help them understand the nature of that power, he reminded them first that it was the power which raised Jesus from death, and second that it was the power which seated him at God's right hand.

As we have seen, however, that does not mean that he is removed far away from us, but it is a picture of various truths which actually make him close and real to us. We thought of the completion of his work of salvation for us, of the comfort which it can bring us to know that he is praying for us, of his cooperation with us in our work for him, and of the consecration which all this demands of us. And now, we can add one more point to the list, the third way in which God's power can be seen and which Paul wants us to know more about. It is Christ's *conquest* over every force or power which would oppose his rule of love. When he raised Christ to his right hand in the heavenly realms, it was 'far above all rule and authority, power and dominion, and every title that can be given, not only in the present age but also in the one to come. And God placed all things under his feet' (Ephesians 1:21–22).

'Far above . . . '. That seems at first to be removing Christ from us once again, doesn't it? But watch carefully! Paul does not say 'far above us'; he says 'far above all rule and authority'. In fact, the list of opposing forces which follows is very like the various 'enemies' which we have been considering and of which we have learned to say that not they but Jesus is Lord.

The passage, then, serves in one sense as a summary. In his conquest, Christ is far above them all; none is in a position to challenge his authority, his right to reign, his victory over everything that drags us away from the experience of the love of God.

If in our individual lives we have drawn near to Christ by faith – no, more, if we are 'in Christ' – then the fact that at his exaltation Christ was raised 'far above' all those enemies ought to bring us peace and encouragement.

However, this passage is more than just a summary of what we have already learned. Paul presses on without a break to relate this truth to the church as a whole. And what he says is quite extraordinary: 'and [God] gave him to be the head over all things to the church' (AV). (I find that this older translation makes the point more clearly than the NIV's 'and appointed him to be head over everything for the church.') 'Head over all things'; yes, that is what we have seen from all that goes before: raised and exalted by the power of God, Christ is indeed head over all things, especially all those enemy forces. Earlier in the same verse, Paul has written that God put 'all things' in subjection under Christ's feet. So, we might like to think of this as a sort of title that Christ has. He is the 'head-over-all-things'.

And now, we read, it is in that character, as head-over-all-things, that God has given him to the church. Given him! Reflect for a moment on the magnificent grace that is revealed here. Here we have a triumphant and exalted Christ, who is seated at the very right hand of God himself, whom God has now 'given' to the church.

THE RISEN CHRIST: GOD'S GIFT TO THE CHURCH!

We as individuals face many threatening forces in our lives, filling us with despair one day and terror the next. So the church throughout the world is often embattled and persecuted, marginalized and ignored. Time and again, her voice and witness have been written off or ignored by an apathetic public. Her death has frequently been predicted, if not in fact proclaimed.

Elsewhere, her stand for the gospel has led to such fierce opposition that she has been driven underground and threatened with physical annihilation. Hers is a chequered history of triumph and abject failure, of growth and decline, of division and weakness. Surely the church as a corporate body has faced and feared the future with quite as much anxiety as we each do as individual Christians.

But here is a word which puts all that in a new light, for she has been 'given' Christ as her head-over-all-things. No longer should we regard the church as merely a human institution. It is not an organizational convenience which can be dispensed with as no longer relevant or as something which has outlived its useful existence. When Jesus told Peter with reference to the church that 'the gates of Hades will not overcome it' (Matthew 16:18), he was able to do so in the light of his own victory over death, Hades and all the malevolent powers of this age and of the world to come.

The church, then, is quite unlike any other human organization or movement, however effective and influential, because it is but a 'body' whose 'head' has already been seen to triumph over the worst opposition that could be thrown at it. The church therefore enjoys a security in every age which rests on the same assured basis as that which the individual believer knows. The 'Lord' of the Christian is the same as the 'head' of the church, each inseparable from the other. The encouragement which we have drawn from this teaching earlier in this book can now be seen to be appropriate to the church as a whole.

How might this reality be more effectively known and taught in the contemporary church, so bogged down, as it often seems to be, in the slough of despond? Clearly not, I suggest, by adopting an aggressive or triumphalist stance, which arrogantly asserts its position. Such an attitude would fly directly in the face of the example of its 'head', from whose victory alone the security stems in the first place. Rather, we need to be reminded that his path to exaltation lay by the way of the cross. It is by following in his footsteps that the church will be most effective in its role as the world's servant. To emphasize this hard but vital truth, we need to return to an earlier point in Paul's prayer in Ephesians 1.

THE BALANCE OF WISDOM AND EXPERIENCE

In verse 17, Paul's first request for his readers was that 'the God of our Lord Jesus Christ, the glorious Father, may give you a spirit of wisdom and revelation, so that you may know him better'. 'Wisdom and revelation': what a glorious balance Scripture again presents us with. We tend to lose it by leaning all our weight on one side or the other.

Wisdom here surely reminds us that we are but the latest in many generations who have known the reality of God. They have written about it in the Bible and elsewhere for our benefit and enrichment. To ponder the lessons and insights of so many saints of God is certainly more than a lifetime's study, but as we persevere in it as best we may, we surely can be said to grow in wisdom. It suggests to me the picture of someone who has drawn deeply from the well of the church's past history. He or she has added to it a new appreciation of truth long known, so that it is not likely to be easily swayed by the upheavals of passing fashion.

But that attractive picture has its reverse side. There is a danger of a cold formalism or an academically dry presentation. How many have left one congregation for another because they have found the first one to be cold and lifeless, even if intellectually faithful to the historic Christian faith?

What seems to be lacking in such cases is 'revelation'. It suggests an immediacy about our knowledge of God, a sense that he is speaking directly to us in our present situation in an authoritative and clear manner. Many congregations in Britain have seen this in recent years, and liveliness frequently follows. This too presents an attractive picture, but also brings dangers of its own. Some people feel left out because they do not sense that the words come over with quite the same divine authority that others claim for them. Others find the approach rather superficial.

And in some cases a one-sided emphasis on certain aspects of the truth gets the whole thing out of balance and so in fact ends up in error. Most blind alleys in the history of the teaching of the church have been because of pressing one aspect of the truth to the point where it crowds out other aspects, rather than because of actual error in the first place.

But what is needed, according to Paul's prayer, is not one or the other, but both together in balance. We need experience checked against accumulated wisdom. Wisdom studies the Scriptures and learns from what godly men and women have written about them down the centuries. So we can build up a robust understanding of what we believe. But understanding needs the impact of revelation to bring it to life in today's world. There is no place for anti-intellectualism, just as there is no place for lifeless orthodoxy.

The church will only grow in its knowledge of God as it learns to combine in fruitful tension the twin strands of 'wisdom and revelation'. In this way alone, I suggest, shall we recapture our appreciation of the truth and the experience of what it means to know Christ as the head of the church, just as the same combination will help each individual believer to learn the truth and experience of the Lordship of Jesus.

15
SOMETHING TO SHOUT ABOUT

So why should 'Jesus is Lord' sound so ominous? Why should our response be so far from the revolutionary joy of the New Testament believers? If we can appreciate what the resurrection means, Jesus' Lordship will not be a threat, but something for us to shout about.

The word 'Lord' occurs in some 717 passages in the New Testament, and of course in this short book we have only looked at a tiny fraction of these. I have tried to concentrate on those places which reflect the particular form of the earliest Christian creed, 'Jesus is Lord'. Even then I have sometimes gone further than just the places where that exact expression occurs, as in the last chapter, for instance.

My motive was the oppressive heaviness with which, in my experience, the Lordship of Christ is usually presented in the church today. I believe that this is far removed from the revolutionary joy of the first Christians as reflected in the pages of the New Testament. As we have examined these passages more closely, I hope that your impression will have coincided with mine when I first began to see things in a new light. In fact this confident affirmation is at the very heart of the Christian good news – the gospel.

It is not something to be tacked on afterwards as a rather underhand device to whip us into line once we have been welcomed freely into the community of the church.

Of course, that does not mean that Christianity has nothing to say about obedience, but it does mean viewing it in a very different way. Some readers may feel that I have somehow undercut the basis for godly living which they have been taught and try to practise. But that in itself is no reason for trying to make the New Testament teach something in a way that is not true to the text. Indeed, it is heartening to me to find that Paul himself met similar criticisms when he set out the comparable message of the free justification of sinners by grace active through faith: 'What shall we say, then? Shall we go on sinning, so that grace may increase?' (Romans 6:1; and cf. Romans 6:15 and Galatians 2:17). His response to such an absurd suggestion remains, but it is worth noting that he does not do it by ramming down his readers' throats the undoubted truth that Jesus is Lord. If preachers today were to take more seriously the ways as well as the content of New Testament teaching, I believe that many would be saved from the state of spiritual double mindedness into which I was once being driven.

In drawing this discussion to a close, there remain two passages which we need to consider. They will not really add anything new in terms of the Lordship of

Jesus, but they both serve to bring it home to us in a personal way, and provide a suitable note on which to finish.

HOW ARE WE SAVED?

The first passage is Romans 10:9, in which Paul tells us in a straightforward way how we can be 'saved': 'If you confess with your mouth, "Jesus is Lord," and believe in your heart that God raised him from the dead, you will be saved.' In the immediate context, Paul is addressing the problem of the status of his Jewish brothers now that Christ, the messiah, has come. But he quickly makes clear that the ground of their acceptance by God is now precisely the same as for Gentiles: 'For there is no difference between Jew and Gentile – the same Lord is Lord of all and richly blesses all who call on him, for, "Everyone who calls on the name of the Lord will be saved" ' (verses 12–13). We may take it, then, that the truth of what he is affirming applies to us all.

Now, in this passage we are told what may at first look like two different conditions which lead to salvation, an open confession that 'Jesus is Lord' and an inward belief that God has raised him from the dead. The two points might seem to have little to do with each other. But in the light of all that we have seen so far, it at once becomes clear that the two phrases are saying the same thing in different ways, and this obviously makes much better sense of the verse. On the one hand we have what a convert (perhaps in baptism) says outwardly as a confession of faith, and on the other the inward belief which naturally gives rise to that confession.

We have repeatedly come back to the fact of the resurrection as the cornerstone of the belief that Jesus is Lord of every rival claim to power and authority over our lives. Whether we are terrified at the prospect of death, dismayed by the impersonal forces which seem to govern so much of our lives, apprehensive about the future or intimidated by other people, whether they are Christians or not, it is in the resurrection that we come to see that Jesus is in fact greater than them all.

By so massive a demonstration of power, God has shown that there is no force on, under or above the earth which can hold him down or overcome him. The empty tomb proclaims that the love of Jesus, shown throughout his life and culminating in his death on the cross, is vindicated. Its final triumph is assured. The resurrection shows that love, not might, is right.

If you believe that in your heart, then it is no step at all, merely a statement of your belief, to confess that Jesus is Lord. Within the fellowship of like-minded believers in the church, you are invited to share with them your confidence that you belong to him, that he is your security, and that now you are at peace. That's what the gospel is all about.

16
JESUS OUR JOY!

Thomas the disciple refused a secondhand belief. He would not swallow untested teaching. But when he met the risen Jesus he cried out spontaneously, 'My Lord!' That was not assent to an article in a creed — it was a cry of gratitude, love and joy.

The story of 'doubting Thomas' at the end of John 20 is well known, and it has brought comfort to countless Christians ever since it was first recorded, for his experience mirrors that of so many of us.

You will remember that he was not present on the first occasion when Jesus showed himself alive to the other disciples. Their excitement on telling Thomas that 'we have seen the Lord!' was not enough to convince him. 'I just can't believe it,' he seems to have said, 'It's too good to be true!' And before we rush to criticize him as being too rationalistic or of wanting 'scientific' proof before he would believe, perhaps we might consider the more charitable line of saying that he was simply not prepared to accept something at second-hand. He was disposed to believe, but he was determined that it should be *his* belief, based on his own experience, not that of somebody else, no matter how reliable their testimony might be.

I remember many years ago being invited to speak

at an Easter houseparty for young people at Matlock, in Derbyshire. One teenager made a great impression on us all. Attractive and very much at the centre of the action, she looked to all the world like a radiant Christian. She played the piano at the sessions, she was first down for the early morning prayer meetings, and so on.

After I had spoken on the last day, she approached me and said she would like a private word. I suggested that it might be more appropriate for her to talk to one of her own leaders, or to one of the other women leaders at the houseparty, but no, she was insistent; she had to talk to me.

Not knowing quite what to expect, I found a room where we could talk quietly and undisturbed. And then the whole thing came pouring out with floods of tears. Her life was a sham. Christianity was the most wonderful thing imaginable, but it was not for her. It was too good for her. She was so happy for all her friends who believed, and indeed she herself believed all the essential truths of the faith, but she was convinced that somehow she would never be accepted. And it was making her miserable.

What could I do? With growing desperation I led her from one promise to another in which Scripture assures us that the gospel is for all, that none who come will be turned away, that God loves us as we are and that he receives us freely in Christ. Yes, she knew all that and it was wonderful, but – it was not for her.

Finally, not knowing quite where to go next, I turned to John 1:12 and read it to her: 'Yet to all who received him, to those who believed in his name, he gave the right to become children of God.'

I shall never forget the next few moments. Her head went down into her hands, and then she looked up at me again with the most beatific smile breaking through her tears that I have ever seen. Without having to be told, I knew in that instant that through the words of that familiar verse she had had her own personal encounter with the risen Christ. He was no longer the saviour, but now her saviour; no longer her parents' Lord, her friends' Lord or anyone else's Lord, but *her* Lord. Head knowledge had become heart knowledge, and with it her life was transformed inwardly. Others in the houseparty might not even have noticed a difference in her as we rejoined them for lunch, but she knew, and I knew, that nothing would ever be the same again for her.

THE JOY OF THOMAS

It was the same for Thomas. He had seen the joy of the other disciples, but he had not personally been present. It was not for him; it was too good to be true. That is no bad frame of mind in which to consider the claims of Christ. The very fact that so many preachers have made the Lordship of Jesus into something which 'religion' at the human level apparently ought to demand, namely a string of rules which we mere mortals should obey if we are to win the favour of the deity, suggests that the truths of the gospel are still too good to be true.

But Jesus did not want it to be so. In his thoughtful grace, he returned a week later to speak with Thomas in particular. Echoing the words with which Thomas had given expression to his difficulties, he invited him to 'put your finger here; see my hands. Reach out your hand and put it into my side. Stop doubting and believe' (John 20:27). By referring to the physical contact that Thomas had desired, it seems as though Jesus was here affirming the continuity of his resurrection body with the person whom Thomas had known. This was not some unrecognized apparition or completely new revelation, but the Jesus whom Thomas had come to know, respect and perhaps even love.

The same, but different! For only a few days before, Thomas had known that Jesus was dead, and death is final. It had been the end, perhaps of a glorious dream, and that had seemed to be that. For Thomas in this condition to experience a direct and undeniable encounter with this same Jesus, now risen, was to blow a hole of resurrection magnitude in his previous world vision. It changed everything, for now he was in the presence of one who transcended death, transformed despair and even treated doubt with gentle good humour. He needed no second invitation or even physical contact. It was an experience like that of the

122

girl at the Easter houseparty. 'Thomas said to him, "My Lord and my God!"'

Of course, the pathway to faith is not always so dramatic, but as we have seen from Romans 10:9 it will surely always have this element about it, that at some point, whether we can identify the time or not, we come to a realization that 'Jesus is Lord – my Lord'. Faith, then, is no blind leap in the dark, though it certainly goes beyond unaided reason alone. Faith is an acceptance of what either slowly or suddenly becomes a conscious realization within us that Jesus is indeed Lord. He has approached us in love and we have only to relax into his welcoming embrace to know rest from a troubled conscience and peace of heart.

THE JOY OF THE LORD'S TABLE

If that is how it all starts, that is also how it continues. Once seen, it is a reality which presses in on us in every circumstance with a joy which I, for one, have discovered never fades. But being human, we have the need for times of particular reflection. We need to re-affirm what has become the central focus of our lives. There is nowhere more appropriate, I suggest, than at the Lord's table.

It is astonishing how frequently the New Testament associates this celebration with Christ as Lord. It is the 'Lord's Supper' for which we come to the 'Lord's table'. Paul 'received from the Lord' how 'the Lord

Jesus, on the night he was betrayed, took bread', and in doing likewise we 'proclaim the Lord's death until he comes'. We take 'the cup of the Lord' and the emblems speak to us of 'the body and blood of the Lord' (all this from 1 Corinthians 10:21 and 11:20–27).

This central act of Christian worship is celebrated in different ways by different traditions. Common to all, however, is inevitably a focus on the death of Christ, the reality of his presence with us now in resurrection power and the anticipation of his coming again. These are the dominant themes of the Lordship of Christ, and they are articulated with precision and dramatic brevity in the triumphal affirmation at the heart of the communion service in the Church of England:

> Christ has died:
> Christ is risen;
> Christ will come again.

17

FIVE YEARS ON

That was all five years ago. And the process of discovery which I have described happened even longer ago than that. The decision to reissue this book has inevitably led the publisher to ask whether I want to change anything or add more.

I sometimes think that only two sorts of Christian are qualified to write about their experiences. At least, that is how it seems from the books which find the widest market. Either I should be able to tell a story of some amazing experience of the power of God which changed my life in a dramatic manner. Or I should have suffered some major personal crisis from which I have emerged as a different person.

Neither of these is true of me, however. My life is far more ordinary than that. During the last five years I haven't changed my job or moved house. I haven't suffered any major illness or the loss of a close family member. The children, of course, have grown older and are at various stages of moving away from home. But apart from that, not a lot has changed.

That, I suspect, is true of many people, and the danger of only reading accounts of the dramatic or spectacular is that the rest of us can easily become discouraged. We get given an over-glamorized picture of the triumphant Christian life and then find that our own experience doesn't match up to it. The results can be serious. Some people try to force God into doing what they think he ought to be doing and come unstuck when he refuses to be bullied. Others romanticize their lives and end up looking and sounding ridiculous to their friends. Others simply give up, thinking they have been conned.

Now of course, I have no objection to reading stories of God's greatness – the Bible too is full of them! But equally we have to realize that life is never going to be like that all of the time, nor, so far as I can see, does the Bible suggest that it is meant to be. What we need, rather, is what might be called a gospel for the ordinary, something through which the reality of God is known even when there are no spiritual fireworks, something which will sustain our devotion and service when the sheer regularities of everyday life might drown them in a sea of apathy.

Well, I've got news for you! The discoveries which I have described in this book have proved to be just such a gospel, and the years which have passed since it was first written have done nothing to dim or diminish it. There is a truth here which was withheld from me for so long but to which I now return time and again with the same settled joy that I recall when it first dawned upon me. To be sure, I have not stood completely still in the meantime, and I know that I still have much to learn. The great thing is, though, that I do so from the sure basis of a gospel which *works*.

This means that we do not have to rely on regular

fixes of the extraordinary to sustain our faith and confidence in God. Rather, just as by his birth Jesus came to share in our common humanity, so he continues to do so today as Lord, transforming the ordinary into a rich experience of his constant love and security. My simple testimony is that this continues to be the case several years on. I trust that the reissue of this book will help you to discover the same.